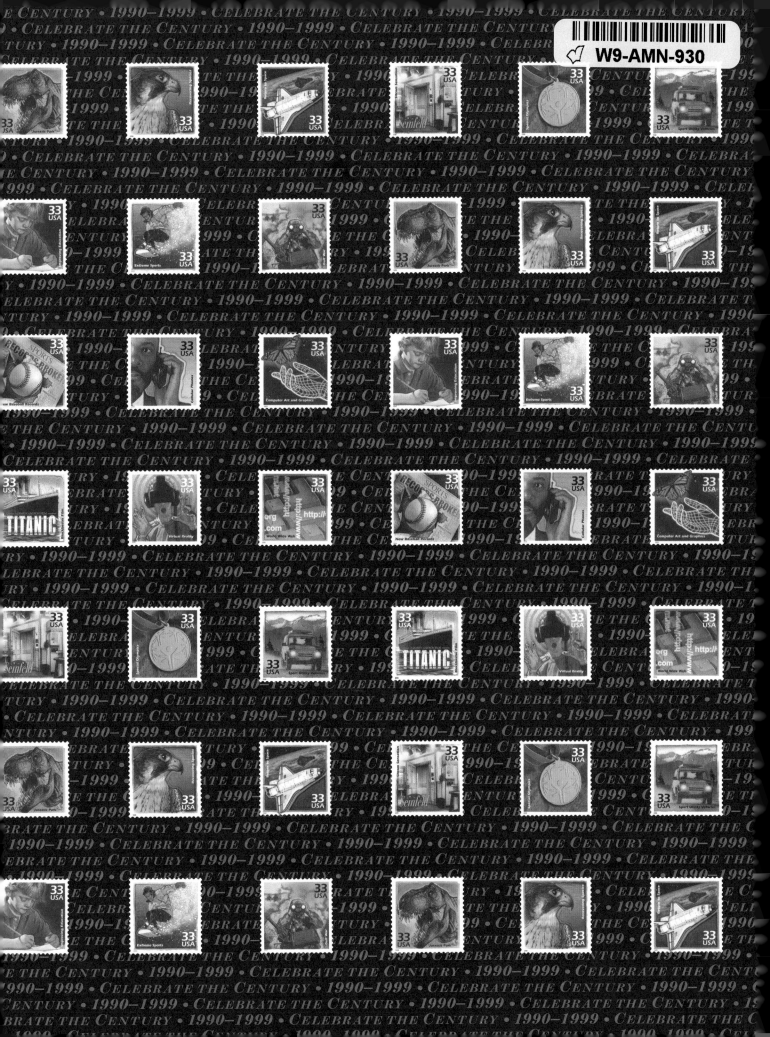

Celebrate THE Century.

A COLLECTION OF
COMMEMORATIVE STAMPS

1990-1999

UNITED STATES POSTAL SERVICE

POSTMASTER GENERAL
AND CHIEF EXECUTIVE OFFICER
William J. Henderson

SENIOR VICE PRESIDENT, GOVERNMENT
RELATIONS AND PUBLIC POLICY
Deborah K. Willhite

VICE PRESIDENT, PUBLIC AFFAIRS
AND COMMUNICATIONS
Azeezaly S. Jaffer

MANAGER, PROMOTIONS
Gary A. Thuro Jr.

PROJECT MANAGER
Clarence R. Williams

TIME LIFE BOOKS

TIME-LIFE BOOKS IS A DIVISION OF TIME LIFE INC.

TIME-LIFE
TRADE PUBLISHING

VICE PRESIDENT AND PUBLISHER
Neil Levin

DIRECTOR OF NEW PRODUCT DEVELOPMENT
Teresa Graham

PROJECT MANAGER
Jennifer L. Ward

PRINTING PRODUCTION MANAGER
Vanessa Hunnibell

EDITORIAL STAFF FOR
CELEBRATE THE CENTURY

MANAGING EDITOR
Morin Bishop

EDITORS
John Bolster, Jeanann Pannasch, Eve Peterson

DESIGNERS
Barbara Chilenskas, Jia Baek

WRITERS/RESEARCHERS
*Ward Calhoun, Theresa Deal,
Jeff Labrecque, Ylann Schemm*

PHOTO EDITOR
Bill Broyles

LIBRARY OF CONGRESS CATALOGING-IN-PUBLICATION DATA
Celebrate the century: a collection of commemorative stamps.
     p.   cm.   Includes index.
Contents: v. 10. 1990–1999
ISBN 0-7835-5326-9
1. Commemorative postage stamps—United States—History—20th century.
2. United States—History—20th century.
I. Time-Life Books

HE6185.U5C45 1998   97–46952
769.56973—DC21   CIP

PICTURE CREDITS

Cover, Stephen Simpson/FPG; 4, Patrick Durand/Sygma; 5, Mathieu Polak/Sygma; 6, Wesley Hitt/Liaison; 7, Superstock; 8, Liaison; 9, Everett Collection; 10, Anthony Suau/Liaison; 11, Sygma; 12, bottom left, Diana Walker/Liaison; inset, Robin Nelson/Black Star; 12-13, Peter Turnley/Corbis; 14, top left, Peter Turnley/Corbis; 14-15, Peter Turnley/Corbis; 15, top right, Sohm/Chromosohm; bottom right, J. Langevin/Sygma; 16, Everett Collection; 17, Merie W. Wallace/20th Century Fox/Photofest; 18, Merie W. Wallace/20th Century Fox/Photofest; 19, Photofest; 20, Photofest; 21, 20th Century Fox; 22, Chuck Burton/AP; 23, Stan Godlewski/Liaison; 24, Paul Warner/AP; 25, left, Corbis/Bettmann-UPI; right, Michael C. York/AP; 26, Special Olympics; 27, top, Chuck Burton/AP; inset, Bill Weems/Special Olympics; 28, Kevin Fleming/Corbis; 29, AGE Fotostock; 30, Elise Amendola/AP; 31, left, Courtesy Yahoo! Inc.; center, Courtesy eBay Inc.; right, Courtesy Condé Nast Publications Inc.; 32, Heath Robbins/FPG; 33, Motorola Museum of Electronics; 34, top right, Jonathan Kirn/Tony Stone Images; bottom left, Motorola Museum of Electronics; insets, Motorola Inc.; 35, top, Dan Loh/AP; insets, Motorola Inc.; 36, top left, Index Stock; center, Gary Holscher/Tony Stone; 37, top right, Tony Arruza/Corbis; bottom right, Superstock; 38, Natalie Fobes/Corbis; 39, George Lepp/Corbis; 40, top, Leonard Lee Rue/FPG; bottom left, Harold E. Malde; bottom right, Rob Badger/FPG; 41, Stan Ololinski/FPG; 42, Kennan Ward/Corbis; center, Jeff Foot/Bruce Coleman; 43, Paul S. Howell/Liaison; 44, Murray Close/Universal City Studios & Amblin; 45, Murray Close/Universal City Studios & Amblin; 46, Photofest; 47, top, Peter Iovino/Universal City Studios & Amblin; bottom, Murray Close/Universal City Studios & Amblin; 48, Murray Close/Universal City Studios & Amblin; 49, top, Murray Close/Universal City Studios & Amblin; bottom, Everett Collection; 50, Icon Sports Media; 51, Stephen Green/*SI*; 52, Walter Iooss Jr/*SI*; 53, inset, Jonathan Kirn/Allsport; right, Vince LaForet/Allsport; 54, V. J. Lovero/*SI*; 55, Walter Iooss Jr/*SI*; 56, Rick Griffiths/Virginia Tech; 57, Sam Ogden/Science Photo Library/Photo Researchers; 58, David Parker/Science Photo Library/Photo Researchers; 59, top, Janet Jensen/*The News Tribune*/AP; bottom, Electric Visualization Lab/University of Illinois at Chicago; 60, Courtesy of General Motors Research & Development Center; 61, top, Electric Visualization Lab/University of Illinois at Chicago; inset, Joe Ellis/AP; 62, Superstock; 63, Martin Goddard/Tony Stone; 64, The Purcell Team/Corbis; 65, Joel W. Rogers/Corbis; 67, Peter Hamblin/The Edison Project; 68, top, Peter Hamblin/The Edison Project; inset, Brooks Kraft/Sygma; 69, Superstock; 70, Steve Liss/Sygma; 71, top, Owen Franklin/Corbis; bottom, Sohm/Chromosohm; 72, Everett Collection; 73, Barry Slobin/Castle Rock; 74, Everett Collection; 75, top, Carin Baer/Castle Rock; bottom, Byron Cohen/Castle Rock; 76, top left, Spike Nannarello/Castle Rock; bottom left, Everett Collection; center, Carin Baer/Castle Rock; 78, Jim Thornburg/Outside Images; 79, VCG/FPG; 80, left, Craig Prentis/Allsport; right, Franco Vogt/Corbis; 81, Adam Pretty/Allsport; 82, top, Richard Price/FPG; bottom, Mike Powell/Allsport; 83, top, Jeff Divine/FPG; bottom left, Mike Powell/Allsport; bottom right, Mike Powell/Allsport; 84, Johnson Space Center/NASA; 85, Tony Ranze/AFP/Corbis; 86, Johnson Space Center/NASA; 87, Kennedy Space Center/NASA; 88, Johnson Space Center/NASA; 89, Johnson Space Center/NASA; 90, Photofest; 91, Everett Collection; 92, Jim Jennings Architecture/Red Melon Studios; 92-93, Rockefeller/Hricak Architects; 93, Index Stock; 94, left, Viewpoint Digital; top right, Daniel Pelavin; 95, Michael Rosenfeld/Tony Stone.

CONTENTS

With the Gulf War (left) won, Americans turned their attention to the far reaches of cyberspace (above).

INTRODUCTION

As they brought the twentieth century and the second millennium to a rousing if not apocalyptic conclusion, the 1990s mixed elements from each of the previous nine decades. From the Roaring Twenties, the '90s borrowed unprecedented economic prosperity, along with a wildly speculative stock market; from the '40s, success in war; and from the '50s, a stymied effort at foreign intervention, this time in Somalia. The life-transforming changes of the industrial revolution in the 1900s resurfaced in futuristic guise in the 1990s' information revolution. Bell-bottoms, the 1970s fashion staple, and '60s hero John Glenn both made comebacks. Laced with contradiction and bookended by economic extremes, the decade formed a kind of retrospective of the twentieth century even as it vaulted America into the future with its own exhilarating advancements.

Developments such as the World Wide Web, virtual reality and human-genome research wrought considerable change in the '90s, but more enticing were the transformations they hinted at. The human genome was nearly mapped by 1999, bringing genetic cures for disease within reach. A geneticist in Scotland cloned a sheep in 1997, hastening the day when, for better or worse, human beings could be cloned. The applications of the World Wide Web, which altered daily life upon its appearance in 1991, were only beginning to be explored at decade's end. No one could say for certain where all the Web's byways would lead, but if the amount of money investors poured into Internet companies during the '90s was any indication, the sky was the limit.

A sky's-the-limit economic mentality had also characterized the 1980s, an era of conspicuous consumption and top-heavy wealth distribution.

Slugger Mark McGwire shattered Roger Maris's home run record and helped reignite the nation's passion for baseball.

Trendwatchers had predicted that the '90s, then, would be a corrective to the decadence of the '80s. People would tire of materialism, the pundits said, and return to spirituality, religion and down-to-earth values. The imminent end of the millennium, with its biblical-apocalyptic implications, would only deepen this impulse.

The experts were right—at the start of the decade, anyway. As if on cue to signal that the 1980s party was over, trouble flared in the Persian Gulf in 1990. Saddam Hussein, the president of Iraq, rolled his forces into the heart of his tiny, oil-rich neighbor, Kuwait, in August. The Iraqi army easily seized Kuwait City and continued west, threatening the border to Saudi Arabia. The offensive created dangerous instability in an economically and politically sensitive region and forced the United States' hand. "This is not an American problem," declared President George Bush. "It is the world's problem."

Indeed it was, but the United States spearheaded the United Nations' response to Hussein's invasion, establishing Operation Desert Shield, a force of 300,000 Allied troops in Saudi Arabia in October 1990. When the action did little to quell Iraqi aggression, Operation Desert Shield was upgraded to Operation Desert Storm, a joint military effort that had the backing of 25 Allied nations, including the United States' Cold War rival, the Soviet Union—a nation on the brink of a historic dissolution at the time.

Like the decade to follow, Desert Storm was all about technology: The United States overwhelmed Iraq with computer-guided missiles, or "smart bombs," that could make surgical strikes from planes, or warships hundreds of miles away. In short order, Baghdad was devastated and the Iraqi communications system crippled. A 100-hour ground war wrapped up Desert Storm slightly more than a month after it began.

While the Gulf War demonstrated America's might and efficiency, and the subsequent breakup of the Soviet Union left the United States as the world's lone superpower, the country still struggled on the domestic front. With the economy in recession, the predicted return to idealism was well within the budgets of most Americans, and religion made a comeback. After a general shift toward secular humanism in the 1960s and '70s, a 1993 poll claimed that eight out of 10 Americans believed in God, more than half attended religious services regularly and 62 percent claimed that religion was an increasingly important influence in their lives.

If Americans were searching for answers, the process was painful at times. Race relations remained complex and problematic. In 1992 four white Los Angeles police officers were acquitted in the videotaped beating of black motorist Rodney King, whom they had arrested after a high-speed chase. When news of the verdict broke, Los Angeles erupted in a full-scale riot. Three days of arson, vandalism and looting left 53 people dead and 2,383 injured. In '94, pro football Hall of Famer O. J. Simpson, an African American, was charged in the murder of his former wife, Nicole Brown, and her acquaintance, Ron Goldman, both white. Riding shotgun in his now-famous white Ford Bronco,

Extreme sports such as snowboarding drew increasing numbers of participants, particularly among the thrill-seeking young.

with a wad of cash and a loaded gun, Simpson led police on a surreal, nationally televised low-speed chase on an L.A. freeway while thousands of people watched and cheered from the roadside. When Simpson was acquitted of murder 16 months later, public response was sharply divided along racial lines: whites were stunned, while blacks celebrated.

The ascendant popular music of the time, grunge, was an angry, angst-ridden hybrid of punk and heavy metal. Its reluctant figurehead, Kurt Cobain of the Seattle-based trio Nirvana, committed suicide in April 1994. One year later, a domestic terrorist bombed the Alfred P. Murrah federal office building in Oklahoma City, killing 169 people, including 19 children, and wounding many more. The picture of America in the '90s as a more grounded, spiritual place was so far failing to come into focus.

But seeds of change were beginning to sprout. In 1991 Tim Berners-Lee, a British physicist working in Geneva, had released the World Wide Web, a computer linking system that he had been developing since 1980, to the general public. The Web's primary feature was "hypertext," words and phrases in a document that could be "clicked on" by a computer mouse to connect to other, related documents. Hypertext could link computers to one another in an unending chain. Once turned over to the public, the Web could expand infinitely.

Berners-Lee declined to capitalize commercially on his invention, which he envisioned as a tool for corporate and social interaction. In early 1993 two computer engineers from the University of Illinois named Marc Andreessen and Eric Bina introduced Mosaic, a browser for the Web that quickly became the most widely used "search engine" on the ever-expanding medium. In the wake of Mosaic's success, the pair launched a company named Netscape, with a revamped commercial browser as its flagship product. Sixteen months later, Netscape went public in the fourth-largest initial public offering in history. By the end of the frenzied day of trading, all five million Netscape shares up for

Stunning special effects and a story of forbidden love attracted record-breaking numbers of moviegoers to James Cameron's *Titanic*.

sale had been purchased, and the company, which had yet to turn a profit, was worth $2 billion.

Other companies, such as Internet access provider America Online and search-engine specialist Yahoo!, quickly joined the fray and the high-tech boom was on. In January 1993 fewer than 50 Web sites existed. Five years later the Web counted an estimated 1.8 million sites. Roughly three percent of U.S. public schools were connected to the Internet in 1994. Four years later that figure rocketed past 50 percent. People used the Internet for a wide range of purposes, from socializing in so-called "chat rooms" to conducting research to corresponding through electronic mail, or e-mail, whose volume soon dwarfed that of traditional mail—which Web denizens quickly dubbed "snail mail." But the primary fuel for the Web explosion was commerce. Online consumer spending hit $8.2 billion during the 1998 Christmas season. Business-to-business e-commerce totaled $7 billion in 1999, and one expert predicted that figure would top $325 billion by 2002. An estimated 58 million people used the Web in '98, with thousands more connnecting every day.

The high-tech boom hot-wired the U.S. economy and led to the largest expansion in its history. Unemployment and inflation dipped to all-time lows. When President Bill Clinton ran for reelection in '96 voters declined to rock the boat of prosperity: Clinton easily defeated Republican senator Bob Dole, and the economy continued its dizzying ascent.

Just like that, it seemed, the nation shed its malaise. The Soviet Union was long gone, Europe was struggling toward a common market and currency, and Asia, long an economic powerhouse, was in the grip of a recession. The world had been remade. Information was its new currency, and the United States its undisputed leader.

Chattering on cell phones, speeding to and fro in sport utility vehicles (SUVs)—often at the same time—Americans were flush with prosperity and eagerly navigating the information superhighway. They also focused on issues that in tougher times had been relegated to the background. Education reform and environmental concerns, such as the protection of endangered species, returned to the fore. Baseball, whose star was dimmed considerably by a 1994 players' strike, reclaimed its role as the national pastime. Cal Ripken's 1995 pursuit of Lou Gehrig's legendary "Iron Man" record and Mark McGwire and Sammy Sosa's captivating 1998 chase of Roger Maris's single-season home run record helped resurrect the game.

Perhaps because the fabric of daily life was so unruffled by crime or hardship, Americans sought physical thrills in record numbers. So-called extreme sports—adrenaline-junkie pursuits such as bungee jumping, sky diving and snowboarding—boomed as never before. Blockbuster films enjoyed a renaissance: In 1993 Steven Spielberg's dinosaur thriller *Jurassic Park* bounded off with a $913-million box-office take in its toothy jaw. That was nothing compared to 1997's *Titanic*, a $200-million epic directed by James Cameron, which despite hitting a few critical icebergs grossed $1.8 billion worldwide.

On television, *Seinfeld,* a witty and inventive sitcom that purported to be "about nothing," became the decade's smash hit. Giddy, absurd and unburdened by moral dilemmas or lessons learned, *Seinfeld* matched the late-decade mood exactly. A renewed self-assurance settled over America.

But there had been embarrassments and hints of darkness along the way. Shootings at public schools plagued the decade. Nightmarish scenes in which young boys suddenly turned on their classmates with guns occurred from Arkansas to Oregon. The worst of these came in 1999, when a pair of teenagers in Littleton, Colorado, armed themselves to the teeth and carried out a murderous rampage at their high school one April morning, killing 13 people before taking their own lives.

President Clinton narrowly escaped political death in 1998 after lying about a sporadic affair he had carried on with 21-year-old White House intern Monica Lewinsky. The scandal obsessed the nation's media—and the office of special prosecutor Kenneth Starr—for all of '98 and ended in a Senate trial that

The ensemble cast of *Seinfeld* brought a new brand of quirkiness to prime-time TV.

saw Clinton impeached but not removed from office.

The high-tech revolution encountered a few glitches as well. As the year 2000 approached, the so-called Y2K problem, which some quarters insisted would be catastrophic, commanded center stage. Since most of the world's computers had been programmed to recognize years by two digits instead of four, it was feared the machines would read the year 2000 as 1900 and crash or churn out unreliable data as a result. With worldwide systems from banking to air-traffic control to sewage disposal controlled by computers, widespread crashes could have been disastrous. Programmers scrambled throughout 1998 and '99 to adapt the technology. Fears of the Y2K problem, so prominent in the waning months of 1999, were largely forgotten after New Year's Day, 2000, passed almost without incident.

Americans resumed their jaunty pace, and the economy, happily locked into what Federal Reserve chairman Alan Greenspan called a "virtuous cycle," continued to grow without inflation. No one knew, and few cared to wonder, when the bubble would burst.

GULF WAR

"A line has been drawn in the sand."

With those words, President George Bush committed American military, political and economic might to ejecting Iraqi forces from the tiny oil-producing nation of Kuwait. That commitment drew the United States into the 43-day Gulf War in 1991, a conflict that redefined the nature of modern warfare, changed the way the media covered war and solidified America's position as a global police force in the post–Cold War era.

On August 2, 1990, six days prior to Bush's declaration, forces led by Saddam Hussein, the president of Iraq, steamrolled across Kuwait's northern border. The Iraqi war machine also moved west, threatening the Saudi Arabian border.

Bush did not hesitate. "This is not an American problem or a European problem or a Middle East problem," the president told the country on August 8. "It is the world's problem."

He outlined America's policy with four objectives: force Iraqi troops to withdraw from Kuwait, restore the Kuwaiti government, maintain the security and stability of the Persian Gulf region and protect American lives. Enforcing the objectives would not be easy. Iraq was not a Panama or Grenada—two small countries against which the United States had waged weekend-wars in the 1980s. Hussein deployed one of the largest and most experienced armies in the world. After nearly a decade of brutal war against Iran in the 1980s, Iraqi troops and commanders were no strangers to desert warfare.

Above all, though, the United States and its allies feared that Iraq would employ weapons of mass destruction. Hussein had both biological and nuclear weapons programs, and in the past he had demonstrated a willingness to use chemical weapons. In 1988 he gassed his own people to quell a rebellion among the Kurds in Halabja.

The sky above Baghdad was ablaze with firepower (above), but American troops (left) saw little action on the ground.

Still haunted by the ghosts of Vietnam, many Americans cringed at the thought of sending men and women into battle halfway around the world. But Bush succeeded in convincing Congress and the United Nations that Hussein must be stopped.

The UN responded by imposing economic sanctions and authorizing "necessary measures," including military action, to enforce them. Operation Desert Shield was under way: By October, 25 Allied nations had deployed approximately 300,000 military personnel in Saudi Arabia. Even the Soviet Union, a U.S. adversary for half a century, stood against Iraq.

But Saddam Hussein would not budge. He established a puppet government in Kuwait, threatened to use Western hostages as human shields and promised to bomb Israel in response to any U.S.-led attack. "Should the Americans become embroiled, we will make them swim in their own blood," he proclaimed.

As Iraq prepared for a ground confrontation, more Allied troops poured into Saudi Arabia. The UN set a January 15 deadline for all Iraqi troops to withdraw from Kuwait. When that date approached without any progress, it became apparent there would be no peaceful resolution.

Operation Desert Storm, which began in the early hours of January 17, 1991, introduced the world to a numbing, strangely antiseptic type of

Saddam Hussein (inset, with a young hostage) visited mass destruction on northern Kuwait (above), as his forces fled the country under increasing pressure from the forces led by President Bush (left) and generals Colin Powell and Norman Schwarzkopf (right).

12

warfare dominated by sophisticated air power, rather than ground forces. Computer-guided missiles, launched from warships and dropped from stealth aircraft, devastated Baghdad and Iraqi military installations, often with near surgical precision. Within 48 hours, the Iraqi military leadership was rendered deaf, dumb and blind as "smart bombs" eliminated strategic communication sites throughout Iraq. Before long, the only information coming out of Baghdad was courtesy of CNN, the American 24-hour cable news station.

CNN's 'round-the-clock coverage of the war revolutionized the relationship between television and combat. When the first bombs rained down on Baghdad, CNN's cameras relayed live images of the night sky brightened by incoming missiles and outgoing antiaircraft artillery. CNN correspondents such as Bernard Shaw and Peter Arnett brought the war into living rooms around the world.

As a result Americans became familiar with the roles and personalities of General Norman Schwarzkopf, Chairman of the Joint Chiefs of Staff General Colin Powell, Secretary of Defence Dick Cheney and Iraqi Foreign Minister Tariq Aziz. They knew about Iraq's Scud missiles and the United States' Patriot antimissile system. As CBS producer Don Hewitt said, "When there was a disaster, it used to be that people went to church

"He is neither a strategist ... nor is he a tactician, nor is he a general, nor is he a soldier. Other than that, he's a great military man."

—GENERAL H. NORMAN SCHWARZKOPF, when asked for his impressions of Saddam Hussein as a military strategist

Returning U.S. troops received a hero's welcome (opposite top) after helping end Hussein's action against Kuwait that left oil fields burning (above) and made refugees of hundreds (right) but stopped short of the chemical warfare the Allies had feared and prepared for (opposite, bottom).

and held hands. . . . Now the minute anything happens they all run to CNN."

Bush called a cease-fire on February 28, after a 100-hour ground war. The "mother of all battles" that Hussein promised and the Allies feared never materialized. Most Iraqi troops, shellshocked from prolonged air bombardment, surrendered en masse soon after Allied troops engaged them. While fewer than 150 American soldiers lost their lives, the *New York Times* wrote that a conservative estimate of Iraqi dead was 100,000.

As Iraq retreated from Kuwait, some military and political observers suggested that Bush had stopped the fighting too soon. After all, Hussein was still in power. But the mission, as Bush and his advisers saw it, had been completed: Iraq was out of Kuwait, Israel had been kept out of the war and the U.S.-led coalition was preserved.

Despite the second-guessing, Bush and the country emerged triumphant. The president's approval rating soared to 91 percent, the highest ever, and the U.S. had made strides to overcome the painful legacy of Vietnam.

14

Aftermath

Despite crippling economic sanctions, Saddam Hussein survived his defeat and tightened his grip on power in Iraq. He brutally put down postwar rebellions and quickly went to work rebuilding his war machine. His open defiance of UN resolutions and insistence on developing weapons of mass destruction resulted in numerous crises and brought more ruin upon Iraq in the years that followed.

In the United States, President Bush seemed certain to ride the wave of postwar adulation to reelection in 1992. But his bid for a second term was derailed by a sluggish economy and a slick Arkansas governor.

15

TITANIC

"Are you ready to go back to *Titanic*?" asks treasure hunter Brock Lovett of 101-year-old Rose Calvert, fictional survivor of the most famous shipwreck in history. Rose's affirmative reply was echoed by millions of moviegoers during the 1997 holiday season and the following months. According to a *Newsweek* poll in February 1998, an astonishing 76 percent of people who had already seen James Cameron's *Titanic* twice said they planned to return to the theater a third time to watch Rose relive her four days aboard the ill-fated ocean liner.

Prior to its maiden voyage from Southampton, England, to New York on April 10, 1912, the 882-foot "ship of dreams" had been declared unsinkable. With a passenger list that included a sizable dollop of high society's cream, the prospect of disaster was in any case unthinkable. Yet the *Titanic* went down within two hours after striking an iceberg. And because the luxury craft carried less than half the number of lifeboats needed to save its more than 2,200 passengers and crew, 1,500 people perished in the frigid waters east of Newfoundland.

The disaster has been attracting "Titaniacs" for decades. In 1987 writer-director James Cameron joined their ranks. After watching the first televised footage of the ship's wreckage on the cable TV program, *National Geographic Explorer*, Cameron jotted down a thumbnail sketch of the future blockbuster. Drawing inspiration from what he saw, Cameron envisioned a love story intertwined with the fascinating details about the ship and her maiden—and only—voyage.

Cameron persuaded the skipper of the Russian ship *Keldysh* to allow him to use the vessel and its two submersibles, *Mir 1* and *Mir 2*, for dives to the wreckage, which lay two and a half miles below the ocean's surface. In 1995, even before the script had been crafted, Cameron participated in 12 dives.

The fictional tale of *Titanic* revolves around a

Thanks to its massive set (above) and stars Leonardo DiCaprio and Kate Winslet (left), *Titanic* was anything but a disaster.

female *Titanic* passenger, her forbidden love and a priceless blue heart-shaped diamond pendant called "The Heart of the Ocean" that is being sought by present-day treasure hunter Lovett (played by Bill Paxton). Seventeen-year-old Rose DeWitt Bukater (played by Kate Winslet), unwillingly betrothed to Cal Hockley (Billy Zane) by her financially strapped widowed mother, wants to be free of the confines of high society, even if it costs her life. While mustering the courage to jump off the ship's bow, she meets Jack Dawson (Leonardo DiCaprio), a vagabond artist who won his passage on the *Titanic* with a lucky hand of poker. A passionate opposite-sides-of-the-tracks affair ensues and the two struggle to survive both as lovers and passengers on the doomed ship. Rose survives, Jack dies and the diamond pendant that Cal had given to Rose presumably goes down with *Titanic*. In present-day sequences, Lovett and his crew enlist the help of an aged Rose (Gloria Stuart), who captivates her audience with her memories of *Titanic*.

As writer, director and film editor, Cameron was vigilant in his efforts to accurately re-create the *Titanic*'s opulence as well as its tragedy. Instead of the Hollywood standard plastic and plaster of paris for props and scenery, Cameron used crystal for the chandeliers, glass for the sconces and real oak for the decks and the Grand Staircase, "the architectural centerpiece of the *Titanic* interior." The ship and the shipyard were re-created (at slightly less than the actual sizes)

> **"*Titanic* is not just a cautionary tale—a myth, a parable, a metaphor for the ills of mankind. It is also a story of faith, courage, sacrifice and, above all else, love."**
>
> —*JAMES CAMERON,*
> *director of* Titanic,
> *1997*

from the original designs at a custom-made studio in Baja, Mexico. The director even had the cast, including the 2,000 extras, attend sessions on nineteenth-century social etiquette. Cameron's drive for authenticity and the elaborate special effects taxed the budget, which ballooned to a record $200 million—a sum that nearly caused the production to sink.

The director's commitment to *Titanic*, however, ran deep. When urged by Twentieth Century Fox to contain spending by cutting scenes, Cameron, who had previously directed six films that grossed more than $1.2 billion, erupted, saying, "If you want to cut my film you'll have to fire me, and to fire me you'll have to kill me!" Heated budget wrangling led Cameron to forfeit his director's fee and "backend deal," or his share of the box-office receipts that would have been worth $10–20 million. He kept the $1.5 million scriptwriting fee.

Titanic premiered on November 1, 1997, at the Tokyo International Film Festival to favorable if not rave reviews. Six weeks later the film opened at 2,674 American theaters and drew nearly $29 million in weekend ticket sales. A surprise overnight sensation, *Titanic* showings sold out hours in advance. Box-office receipts climbed to $88 million

by the second week and reached $100 million after only 12 days. The three-hour, 14-minute epic was on course to surpass *Star Wars* as Fox's most profitable and best loved film ever.

After a strong showing at the Golden Globes in January 1998—eight nominations and four awards, including Best Dramatic Picture and Best Director—*Titanic*'s U.S. box-office totals reached $300 million. Never before had a movie reached that total so quickly. The film received 14 Academy Award nominations—tying the 1950 classic *All About Eve*. Two and a half weeks shy of the Academy Awards ceremony, *Titanic* reached a titanic financial milestone: $1 billion in worldwide ticket sales.

Oscar night proved to be equally monumental: The movie tied 1959's *Ben Hur* with 11 awards, including Best Picture, Best Director, Best Editing and Best Visual Effects. Three of the Oscars went directly to Cameron. During his Best Director acceptance speech he declared, "I'm the king of the world!" parroting Jack Dawson's self-aggrandizing proclamation. In a more thoughtful acceptance for the Best Picture Oscar he said, "The message of *Titanic* is the unthinkable can happen.... The only thing we truly own is today. Life is precious." He closed by requesting a moment of silence for the 1,500 people who died in the *Titanic* disaster during the early morning hours of April 15, 1912.

As *Titanic* began to sink and passengers scrambled into lifeboats (opposite), Winslet's Rose (above, right) waded through the flooded dining room with her lover, Jack, played by DiCaprio (above, left).

Aftermath

The film itself wasn't the only winner. *Titanic*'s theme song, "My Heart Will Go On," sung by pop diva Celine Dion, won the Academy Award for Best Song, and the movie soundtrack, with music composed and conducted by James Horner, sold 10 million copies.

A February 1998 poll indicated that 45 percent of women under age 25 who had seen the movie once returned for a second viewing. The film's Web site received four million hits a day in early 1998, and six *Titanic* books made the *New York Times* bestseller list during a single week. NBC purchased the rights to *Titanic* for $30 million in January 1998, and by December 1999 videotape rentals of the film had topped $300 million. All told, *Titanic* grossed $1.8 billion in worldwide gate receipts.

SPECIAL OLYMPICS

You may remember Geraldo Rivera's landmark 1972 exposé of Staten Island's Willowbrook State School. The horrifying images of mentally handicapped young people, warehoused in unimaginable squalor, shocked the nation and spurred a government inquiry into the institution. The report also prodded the country into adopting a more enlightened view of the mentally handicapped.

A few hundred miles to the south, in Rockville, Maryland, Eunice Kennedy Shriver, sister to President John F. Kennedy, had a head start on that path toward enlightenment. Her older sister, Rosemary, was mentally handicapped, and Eunice knew from observing Rosemary that the mentally handicapped were capable of much more than most people thought. A decade before Willowbrook, Mrs. Shriver began holding summer day camps in her backyard for mentally handicapped adults and

children. As the participants ran, swam, played soccer and rode horses, all with surprising proficiency and a tremendous sense of fulfillment, Mrs. Shriver envisioned a larger stage for these activities. She passionately believed that mentally handicapped persons, young and old, could take part in and benefit from competitive sports.

Toward the end of the '60s a young recreation teacher named Anne Burke (née McGlone) approached the Chicago Park District with an idea for a citywide field day for the mentally handicapped. She was encouraged to present the idea to Shriver, who was then the director of the Kennedy Foundation. Shriver agreed to help, and she greatly expanded the scope of the event, naming it Special Olympics and aiming for international participation.

Mrs. Shriver recruited a legion of volunteers, including 1960 Olympic decathlon gold medalist

The '95 Special Olympics (above) drew athletes from 21 nations, including some fired-up soccer players from Rhode Island (left).

"Let me win. But if I cannot win, let me be brave in the attempt."

—THE SPECIAL OLYMPICS OATH

Helping kick off the first Special Olympics in 1968 were (above, left to right) Bishop David Dempsey, Eunice Shriver, Illinois Lt. Governor Paul Simon and Sargent Shriver; by 1999 the event had expanded to include more than 7,000 athletes competing in a variety of sports from track-and-field (right) to Shoot Around contests (opposite).

Rafer Johnson, and launched the inaugural Special Olympics Games at Chicago's Soldier Field on July 20, 1968. More than 1,000 athletes from 26 U.S. states, Canada and France participated in the event, which featured competition in track-and-field and aquatics.

"I remember that day for one reason," said Tim Shriver, the President and CEO of Special Olympics in 1999 and son of Eunice Kennedy Shriver. "Here these athletes were competing and giving their all in front of 100,000 empty seats at Soldier Field. As much as anything, those empty seats were a reflection of the times and attitudes."

How the times, and more importantly the attitudes, have changed! Spearheaded by Mrs.

Shriver's unerring vision, and thousands of volunteers and supporters, Special Olympics became an organization of international standing and, in the process, helped reshape public perception of the mentally handicapped. The program celebrated its 30th anniversary in July 1998, and in June 1999, Raleigh-Durham, North Carolina, hosted the 10th Special Olympics World Summer Games, which drew more than 7,000 athletes from 150 countries. The participants competed in 19 sports, including powerlifting, gymnastics and golf, with more than 45,000 spectators in attendance.

The program's rise to such Olympian heights was remarkably steady. Each Special Olympics Games has been larger than the one before it. The second

Games, in 1970, attracted 1,500 athletes to Chicago from all 50 U.S. states, France and Puerto Rico. By the time the fourth Games were held, in Mt. Pleasant, Michigan, in 1975, 10 countries were involved, network TV coverage had been secured and plans for a Winter Special Olympics were afoot. Those plans became reality 18 months later in Steamboat Springs, Colorado. Five hundred athletes participated in the first Special Olympics Winter Games and ABC, NBC and CBS all covered the festivities. In 1988 Special Olympics gained official recognition from the International Olympic Committee, and the Opening Ceremonies for the '99 Games were broadcast in prime time on ABC and hosted by comedian Billy Crystal with entertainment from pop-star Stevie Wonder. Today, Special Olympics provides year-round sports training and competition for more than a million athletes around the world.

The movement has come a long way from empty Soldier Field in 1968—and a world away from Willowbrook.

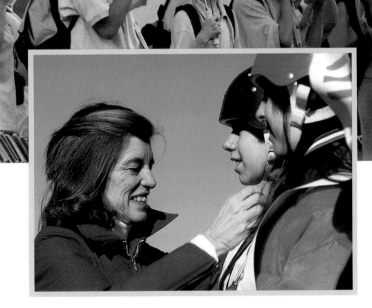

Aftermath

While no individual records are kept at Special Olympics Games, every performance in its history has been impressive, and some have been truly astounding, such as an 11.2-second 100-meter dash and a 4-minute 1500-meter run.

On December 17, 1998, President Clinton and his wife, Hillary, hosted a dinner and reception at the White House to celebrate the 30th Anniversary of Special Olympics. President Clinton closed the evening by saying "This year ... there are more than one million Special Olympics athletes throwing the javelin, swimming the butterfly, walking the balance beam—something most of the rest of us cannot do—and inspiring hope all over the world."

More than 16,000 Special Olympics competitions are staged each year at the local, regional and national levels, and Special Olympics World Games are held every two years, alternating between Summer and Winter Games. The 2001 Special Olympics World Winter Games will be held in Anchorage, Alaska.

WORLD WIDE WEB

Most great inventions start with a person posing a simple hypothetical question. In the early 1980s British physicist Tim Berners-Lee asked himself, "Suppose all the information stored on computers everywhere were linked.... Suppose I could program my computer to create a space in which anything could be linked to anything?" Out of these queries spun an invention called the World Wide Web, which by the end of the 1990s had revolutionized the way people obtained, exchanged and used information—and in the process, the way people lived.

In 1980, while working at CERN, a famous Particle Physics Laboratory in Geneva, Berners-Lee wrote a weblike program called Enquire to keep track of CERN's personnel and its complex information network. Enquire's crucial feature was hypertext—a programming language that allows words and phrases to be "clicked on" by a cursor and a mouse and links the user to other related documents. Hypertext would be a vital part of the World Wide Web as well.

At the time, computers could already share information via the Internet—an infrastructure that connects computers through cables—which had been up and running since the 1970s. People could also communicate over the Internet with electronic mail (e-mail). But there did not yet exist a place where information could be stored and retrieved on a permanent basis. This was where Berners-Lee stepped in.

Using a new personal computer known as the NeXT—NeXT Inc. was started by Apple Computer cofounder Steve Jobs in 1977—Berners-Lee, with the help of several colleagues, transformed Enquire's global hypertext system into the first Web content server (a sort of electronic filing cabinet). Three technical innovations were key: URLs (Universal Resource Locators), which are Web "addresses," HTTP (Hypertext

"Cyber cafés" with Internet access (left) allowed people to socialize while browsing in all directions on the Web (top).

Transfer Protocol), the system by which documents are linked and HTML (Hypertext Makeup Language), the computer language in which most of today's Web pages and documents are written.

Berners-Lee created a crude version of what is now known as a Web browser, a page that directs users in their search for Web sites and information. In 1991, having created the Web and a rudimentary browser, Berners-Lee persuaded CERN to release the Web to the public, thereby allowing everyone to add to and improve upon the creation.

In February 1993 Marc Andreessen and Eric Bina of the National Center for Supercomputing Applications did just that. Their browser, known as Mosaic, instantly became the most widely used search engine. Slightly more than a year later, Andreessen and several friends launched a com-

mercial browser through their new company, Netscape Communications.

While Andreessen and Netscape would reap huge profits from the Web, Berners-Lee shunned commercialization, thinking it would lead to the creation of incompatible browsers that would in turn stunt the growth of the Web. Even a visionary can be wrong. Commercial browsers with names like Yahoo!, Excite and Hot Bot proliferated without introducing incompatibility. And each new venture seemed to raise the standard of graphics and search options. The Web, with its expanding directory of sites and search engines to locate those sites, grew by leaps and bounds.

By the end of the '90s, with an ever increasing portion of the world's population connected to computers, and with the economy booming, the World Wide Web had become a kind of global souk. In a scenario that not too long ago would have made a great premise for a *Twilight Zone* episode, the Web had made it possible for people to meet most of their daily needs without ever leaving home. People needed to only point a cursor and click to buy gro-

> "There was no Eureka! moment. It was not like the legendary Apple falling on Newton's head.... Inventing the World Wide Web involved my growing realization that there was a power in arranging ideas in an unconstrained, weblike way."
>
> —*TIM BERNERS-LEE, on inventing the World Wide Web*

ceries, trade stocks, rent videos, make travel arrangements and communicate with friends and family—all from the comfort of their computer desk chair. Increasing numbers of holiday shoppers in the late '90s entirely bypassed the crush at the mall and the department store by purchasing online.

The global system of links was also a limitless, quick and invaluable source of information, just as Berners-Lee had envisioned. As of 1998 there were 1.8 million Web sites. A person with a serious illness, for instance, could simply type said malady into a search engine to consult medical journals, find out about specialists and research treatment centers. That person could also talk to others with the same illness in a "chat room."

"Chat rooms"—online meeting places—became a hugely popular feature of the Web. People who felt alone in real life could surround themselves with Internet friends or engage in Internet dating. Some Internet aquaintances led to marriage. Even Berners-Lee could scarcely have imagined how his invention would take off, or what the Web would weave in the twenty-first century.

Aftermath

Now head of the nonprofit World Wide Web Consortium in Cambridge, Massachusetts, which maintains technical standards for the Web, Berners-Lee does somewhat lament the Web's tilt toward commerce. "The original goal was working together with others. The Web was supposed to be a creative tool, an expressive tool," said Berners-Lee.

When he first conceived of it, Berners-Lee imagined that one day the Web would be a place of world collaboration, a forum where disparate cultures and people could exchange ideas and technology in the service of a greater good. At the dawn of the twenty-first century, Web software continued to evolve, and it was increasingly easy for people to create and edit their own pages and add links to other sites, so there was still a chance that the rapidly expanding medium would yet fulfill Berners-Lee's hopeful vision.

CELLULAR PHONES

In the early 1990s the sight of someone walking down the street or riding the train while talking on the phone was something of a novelty. By mid-decade such a sight had become common enough to generate a kind of backlash: anti-cell-phone user jokes cropped up in talk-show host monologues, train passengers sneered and har-rumphed at loud-talking riders. At the end of the decade the sight was common enough to pass without comment. Everyone, it seemed, had a cell phone; not just on-the-go businesspersons but high-school kids, grandparents and stay-at-home moms. The day when the cell phone would replace the wireline phone was visible on the horizon.

Cellular service first became available in the United States in 1983, and in only 16 years the total number of subscribers surpassed 70 million. The industry grew by 25 percent in 1998 alone, and observers predicted that by the end of 2000 there would be more than 100 million cellular subscribers, more than one-third of the nation's population.

The roots of this communications revolution stretch back to mid-century, when the Mobile Telephone Service (MTS), a phone system for cars, appeared in Chicago. Functioning like a two-way radio, the MTS phone was a simplex connection, meaning users had to hold down a button when they wanted to speak and release it when they wanted to listen. The phone also required a suitcase-sized transceiver that fit in the trunk of the car. To phone someone, users connected to an operator, who placed the call for them.

For all the industry's accelerated growth in the late 1990s, progress in the early days was slower than dialing overseas on a rotary phone. The MTS system remained unchanged until 1962, when the catchingly named Improved Mobile Telephone Service (IMTS) debuted, its sole improvement being that the operator was

As cell phones became more compact (above), they could accompany users anywhere, including on a biking trip (left).

The perfect accessory for the fast-paced world typified by stock-market traders (right), cell phones evolved considerably from Motorola's pre-cellular, portable radio telephone (below); in the late '90s they became fashion statements (insets) and caused public pay phones (opposite) to go increasingly unused.

PORTABLE RADIOTELEPHONE SYSTEM

The DYNA T•A•C portable radiotelephone system makes available for the first time a truly portable radiotelephone. It is designed for use by the general public and many other traditional land mobile users.

Incorporating a pushbutton dial, it is as easy to operate as any telephone. Small and lightweight, it provides an instant communications link for the person on the go.

System Features

DYNA T•A•C stands for "Dynamic Adaptive Total Area Coverage." It incorporates high power transmitters and receivers located in clusters of 4 to 6 in a perimeter around each transmitter. This network is interconnected to the land line telephone network via a computer.

Expandable To Meet Market Demands

The DYNA T•A•C portable radiotelephone system starts with a small central core. As the market demand grows the system is expanded outward, and the central core becomes denser. Coverage is controlled so that a large number of users can share the same frequency, conserving spectrum.

The diagrams show two stages in the implementation of a DYNA T•A•C portable radiotelephone system for New York City which illustrates the expandability of the system.

System Flexibility

The system is readily adaptable to the geographic boundaries of any metropolitan area. Geographic re-use of frequencies is permitted as controlled by the DYNA T•A•C portable radiotelephone system coverage concept.

DYNA T•A•C
Portable Radio Telephone System

"By 2010, there will be more than 1.45 billion cellular subscribers worldwide. The number of wireless subscribers will outnumber wireline counterparts by about half a billion."

—BELL LABS RESEARCH, 1999

removed from the equation, and users could now place the calls themselves. The units were still as bulky as foot-lockers. And like their predecessor, they functioned like a scanner: If you held down a channel button you could eaves-drop on other conversations.

The need for privacy and expanded capacity drove the next round of innovations, which included additional channels and duplex capa-bility, a feature that allowed callers to talk and listen at the same time. Still, progress came slowly, and it wasn't until 1983 that the first commercial cellular service was offered. The primary reason for the delay was lack of capacity, or cell sites, around the nation. Cell sites consist of a tower with an antenna on top and a computer at the base. They are called cells because they emit frequencies in concentric circles like a cross section of a biological cell, or rings on a pond.

When a call is placed from a wireless phone, communica-tion rides radio waves to a cell site, which tran-

fers the call by wires or microwaves to the mobile telephone switching office (MTSO), the catalyst of the system. The MTSO then sends the call on wires to the local telephone company, which treats the call like any other. If a call is being made from one cell phone to another, it is beamed from the MTSO directly to the second party's phone. The FCC designated radio spectrum for cellular use in 1974, but it took seven years for each of the country's 306 service areas to acquire a carrier.

Progress, to say the least, has picked up speed since then. In 1999 the number of people signing up for cellular service daily was estimated at 30,000. Cellular technology is able to accommodate such large numbers of users because the cells, which subdivide a given region, transmit at a low enough power to allow for frequency reuse. That is, a single frequency can be used simultaneously by different cells in a calling area. Additionally, a single cell uses only a fraction of the channels available to it, leaving plenty of room for other callers.

The number of subscribers and the number of cell sites continue to increase in lockstep, ensuring that one day in the not-so-distant future we will look back with nostalgia at the quaint wireline phones of the twentieth century.

By the end of the 1990s, cellular phones had burst out of the briefcase and into almost every aspect of everyday life: Calls could be taken on the golf course (opposite), during a break on the farm (left), on college campuses (below) and while lounging on the beach (above).

Aftermath

At the turn of the century cell phone technology was still rapidly evolving. Cell phones came in three categories: Personal Communications Systems (PCS), Cellular and Nextel. Each category used a different frequency and there were seven types of digital technologies spread among them. Satellite phones sent signals to a communications satellite orbiting 1,000 to 22,000 feet above Earth, which relayed the call to a local phone system and made transcontinental wireless calls possible.

As consumers struggled to sort out the myriad options, other wireless gadgets emerged to further increase their choices. Palm Pilots—handheld computers that came with antennae and could connect to the Internet from almost anywhere—appeared, as did cell phones that could also go online. The days of wireless personal computers seemed to be fast approaching.

RECOVERING SPECIES

For one species to mourn the death of another is a new thing under the sun. The Cro-Magnon who slew the last mammoth thought only of steaks.... The sailor who clubbed the last auck thought of nothing at all. But we, who have lost our [passenger] pigeons, mourn the loss.

— Aldo Leopold, conservationist

Once the most common bird on Earth, the passenger pigeon was hunted into extinction by 1914— a poignant symbol of man's awesome destructive power. A quarter century later another bird, the whooping crane, teetered on the threshold of extinction. At the close of the twentieth century, the fate of the elegant, long-legged bird was still uncertain, but its plight had inspired the United States's first large-scale effort to protect endangered species and led to the passage of the Endangered Species Act (ESA) in 1973. The law mandated that each and every species that was declared endangered be saved.

Since ESA, the U.S. Fish and Wildlife Service (FWS), which enforces the law, has helped save the brown pelican, the California gray whale, the American alligator and the arctic peregrine falcon. And by the end of the 1990s, the gray wolf and the bald eagle were well on the road to recovery. But the cost of saving individual species has been high and the results limited. Birds, like the whooping crane, can be bred in captivity but may or may not make it in the wild. Salmon can be loaded in tanks and trucked upstream to avoid dams but will still face declining populations.

Of all the threats to species survival—from overkill and pollution to introduced species— habitat destruction is the most insidious. For decades, FWS's recovery efforts yielded numerous small, unconnected habitat areas that might help one species but do little for the overall ecosystem. In the early 1990s, though, scientists and environ-

Thankfully, whale watchers (left) can still glimpse the magnificent flukes of the once endangered California gray whale (above).

39

The arctic peregrine falcon (right) and the American alligator (opposite) are two species that have bounced back from the brink of extinction; pockets of Minnesota's Nerstrand Woods (below) have been preserved, but most of the forest, which once covered much of the northern Midwest, has fallen to clear-cutting, a practice that has also ravaged parts of the Olympic National Forest (below, right).

"Floridians have spent most of the 20th century trying to destroy the Everglades, and much of it trying to save the Everglades, often at the same time."

—LAWTON CHILES, governor of Florida, 1991

mentalists began to recognize that preserving biodiversity was more important than saving any one individual species, and that biodiversity required large, contiguous parcels of land. The idea was simple. But if the mating grounds of the black-capped vireo came up against the need for new housing in a growing community, things could still get complex, particularly if the land was privately owned. Acrimony between conservationists and landowners, who were expected to shoulder the economic burden of compliance with ESA, ran high. One landowner in the Southeast, for example, clear-cut a swath of long-leaf

pine forest to prevent the endangered red-cockaded woodpecker from nesting. Another bulldozed a stand of San Diego mesa mint days before the plant was to be added to the ESA list.

Fortunately, a new paradigm for ecosystem preservation began to emerge in the 1990s, one that has brought environmental organizations and industry together as partners. Chevron and World Wildlife Fund might appear to be strange bedfellows, but the oil giant and the conservation group joined forces in the late '90s. Chevron recognized that sound environmental practices were good for public relations—and often cheaper in

the long run—and World Wildlife Fund realized it could advance its cause more effectively with Chevron as a friend rather than an adversary. Similar partnerships took shape in the timber and fishing industries. The Forest Stewardship Council (FSC), made up of loggers and environmentalists, was established in 1993. With input from both parties, the council drafted a list of species- and habitat-friendly logging practices. If timber companies followed the guidelines, they would be "certified" by the FSC, a designation that would make their products more appealing to eco-conscious consumers.

The encroachment of humans on wild animals' habitats—as evidenced by an elk that wandered into a Yellowstone National Park building area (above)—is at the root of all species' endangerment; the brown pelican (left), once in jeopardy, made a complete recovery, while the whooping crane (right) continued its tenuous journey back from the edge of extinction.

At the same time, a series of amendments to the Endangered Species Act allowed the FWS, which enforces the ESA, to shift its focus from fines and jail sentences to incentives as a way to get landowners to help stem species loss. Provisions like habitat-conservation plans, the "safe harbors" policy and the "no surprises" policy were less adversarial and encouraged landowners and businesses to voluntarily implement conservation measures. But with 356 animals and 578 plants listed as endangered in 1999, even a revamped ESA could not hope to save every species.

Homo sapiens have been nudging birds, reptiles, fishes, insects, plants and fellow mammals toward extinction since the end of the Ice Age. By some estimates, more than 90 percent of all species that have ever existed on Earth no longer do.

According to renowned Harvard biologist Edward O. Wilson, 27,000 species worldwide disap-

Aftermath

Public awareness of endangered species continued to grow as the year 2000 dawned, and programs such as Partners for Wildlife and Partners in Flight successfully encouraged conservation efforts among government agencies, individuals, private businesses, industry organizations and groups like the National Audubon Society and the National Fish and Wildlife Foundation. Millions of acres of land were protected for the recovery of struggling species by organizations such as The Nature Conservancy, Trust for Public Land and Wildlife Habitat Council.

In 1999, two pairs of whooping cranes in the United States laid the first eggs in the wild in decades. The four-year-old cranes, which were part of an experimental flock that was raised in captivity, lifted hopes that the birds could make a comeback. From 1993—when officials started sending whooping cranes raised in captivity to Florida—to 2000, a total of 178 of the birds were released.

pear every year—a pace at least 1,000 times greater than the natural rate of species loss. Other sources estimate the rate to be only 10 times greater. In either case, trying to save each and every species would be a Sisyphean task at best. But not to save as many as possible would be cynical and shortsighted. The potentiality that a rare lichen might one day offer a cure for disease is just one reason that preservation is worthwhile. But even more important, animals and plants are inex-

tricably tied to the ecosystem, which is further impoverished by the disappearance of each species.

Undoubtedly, human beings will continue to build roads, shopping malls and houses. They will continue to pollute rivers and introduce alien species that will drive out native ones. But with the passenger pigeon as a reminder of what we have lost, and the whooping crane as a reminder of what we stand to lose, we can hope to slow the race to extinction.

JURASSIC PARK

Director Steven Spielberg promoted his 1993 film about dinosaur resurrection as "science eventuality" rather than science fiction. The story's elements were alarming: blood-engorged mosquitoes, extracted dino DNA, missing genetic sequences, frozen embryos, incubated crocodile eggs. But to the millions who flocked to see Universal Studios and Amblin Entertainment's *Jurassic Park* that summer, it seemed entirely plausible that creatures who had roamed the earth some 65 million years ago could be cloned from surviving DNA fragments.

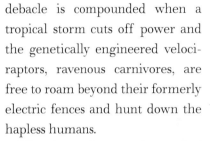

Adapted from Michael Crichton's 1990 techno-thriller novel of the same name, *Jurassic Park* begins with the discovery of dinosaur DNA miraculously fossilized in a mosquito trapped in amber. Mr. Hammond, a child- and dinosaur-loving multimillionaire, has an idea of how to use it. He mobilizes an army of investors, genetic engineers, computer experts and theme park authorities to create a prehistoric park inhabited by genetically engineered dinosaurs. He builds his park, but he can do little to stop the chaos that ensues when a corrupt computer programmer (Wayne Knight of *Seinfeld* fame) sabotages the park's security system to steal dinosaur embryos for a rival company. The debacle is compounded when a tropical storm cuts off power and the genetically engineered velociraptors, ravenous carnivores, are free to roam beyond their formerly electric fences and hunt down the hapless humans.

Were it not for a crack squad of experts in live-action animatronics and computer animation, and the visionary talents of Spielberg, *Jurassic Park* might have been a B monster movie. Instead, Spielberg spent two years in preproduction to lay the groundwork for the film's extraordinary special effects. Designer Stan Winston and his team of 60 artists, engineers and puppeteers spent an entire year researching six of the novel's original 15 species. They worked closely with scientists such as Jack

Spielberg (above) created one of film's most terrifying creatures in the ravenous, rampaging T-Rex (opposite).

Horner, curator of paleontology at the Museum of the Rockies in Bozeman, Montana, to capture the movement patterns and habits of the Velociraptor, Tyrannosaurus Rex, Dilophosaurus, Gallimimus, Triceratops and Brachiosaurus.

The design team used one-fifth scale models to create daunting, lifelike creatures such as the 40-foot-long, 9,000 pound T-Rex. His fiberglass frame was stuffed with 3,000 pounds of clay, wrapped with latex skin and mounted on a "dino

simulator" that was powered by hydraulics and controlled by computer. Other *Jurassic Park* miracles were achieved by George Lucas's Industrial Light & Magic company, which had been created 18 years earlier to handle the special effects for *Star Wars*. When Spielberg saw a herd of stampeding gallimimus created by the new "morphing effect" graphics used in *Terminator 2: Judgment Day*, he "just went nuts," said Dennis Muren, a seven-time Academy Award winner for special effects. Three-

Before the horror sets in and creatures such as the raptor (left) begin running wild, paleontologist Alan Grant (played by Sam Neill) enjoys feeding a docile brachiosaur (opposite), and park founder and visionary John Hammond (played by Sir Richard Attenborough) thrills to the birth of a velociraptor (below).

> "Already there's a kind of misplaced concreteness. Folks, there are no dinosaurs! Just because you saw something that's totally persuasive, they're not there. And genetic engineering is not about to make them."
>
> —*MICHAEL CRICHTON*,
> Jurassic Park *author, in a 1993 interview*

dimensional scans were made from the scale models to create data templates. Perspective was created by "brushing" shadows in some 16.7 million shades (all of which helped create the rippling effect on the animals' skins as they walked). The film's brilliance lay in the seamless integration of computer graphics, large models and live action.

With a $65-million production budget and an estimated $40-million advertising budget, *Jurassic Park* was a bonafide blockbuster. In its mammoth-sized marketing campaign, there were more than 3,000 *Jurassic Park* tie-in products ranging from dino dolls to T-shirts, mugs, video games, candy, trading cards, underwear, board games and McDonalds' Happy Meal Toys. The film grossed $913 million worldwide, and it wasn't only the general public that was amazed. Paleontologists praised the movie's verisimilitude. As UC-Berkeley

professor Mark Goodwin put it, "It looks like they trained a bunch of dinosaurs to be in the movies." Jacques Gauthier, curator for reptiles at the California Academy of Sciences said, "I got a call from a colleague in Michigan…. He was telling me about this scene with several brachiosaurus, and a herd of parasaurolophids, moving along a lakeshore. It was so real he wanted to sit and watch them for a couple of hours to study their behavior."

In the classic Spielberg tradition, *Jurassic Park* appealed to young and old alike. The film is a vividly etched fantasy as well as a cautionary tale that poses increasingly relevant questions: Should scientific knowledge be used to alter nature? What happens when big business co-opts science for its own purposes? In a 1993 interview, Crichton issued his *fin de siècle* warning: "Biotechnology and genetic engineering are very powerful. The film suggests that [science's] control of nature is elusive. And just as war is too important to leave to the generals, science is too important to leave to scientists. Everyone needs to be attentive."

We may not be on the verge of re-creating dinosaurs, but it's important to consider the possible consequences of genetic engineering. And in Spielberg's hands, it's also loads of fun.

Tim Murphy (played by Joseph Mazzello) cowers as raptors pursue him in a memorable kitchen sequence (opposite); key personnel included Spielberg (top, setting up a scene, and above, middle), Attenborough (above, left) and director of photography Dean Cundey (above, right).

Aftermath

In the remaining years of the decade, dinomania went from being the sole province of scientists and curious children to a ravenous general public. Their newfound zeal proved a double-edged sword for scientists. On the one hand, the publicity was good for museums, but on the other, it caused amber prices to skyrocket worldwide and an international market for dinosaur fossils to spring up almost overnight. What began as a slow trickle of curiosities in 1993 became a flood of teeth, bones and entire skeletons by 1997, when the sequel *The Lost World: Jurassic Park* hit the cinemas. Dinosaurs had become big business: Digs on fossil-rich federal lands in the American West were routinely plundered, private landowners would only grant digging rights for exorbitant sums and the number of commercial collectors rose from 10 to 120, many of whom used bulldozers to achieve their ends. Matters came to a head in 1997 when "Sue," a 65-million-year-old T-Rex skeleton—the largest and most complete fossil of that species ever found—was sold to the highest bidder (McDonalds, Disney and the Field Museum of Natural History in Chicago) for $8.3 million.

NEW BASEBALL RECORDS

The underachieving St. Louis Cardinals were 21 1/2 games out of first place by the first week of September 1998. But baseball fans in the city of St. Louis were hardly in a somber mood. In fact, on September 8, 49,987 fans packed Busch Stadium for the Cards game against the Chicago Cubs. The sellout crowd hoped to participate in a memorable slice of baseball history.

In the fourth inning, with a snap of his powerful wrists, Cardinals' first baseman Mark McGwire served up that bit of history. He poked a sinking fastball from Cubs pitcher Steve Trachsel over the left-field wall for his 62nd home run of the season. McGwire was known for his towering, tape-measure blasts, but this one barely cleared the fence. It traveled the shortest distance of any round-tripper McGwire would hit that season, but it was certainly his biggest home run ever. The blast broke Roger Maris's 37-year-old single-season home run record.

McGwire's shot placed an exclamation point at the end of a four-year span that saw baseball reestablish itself as the nation's favorite pastime. A players' strike in 1994 had alienated fans, forced the cancellation of the World Series and endangered the future of the game. By the time the players and owners finally came to an agreement in March 1995, many observers believed the game was doomed and questioned whether the fans had been permanently alienated. Not since the "Black Sox" World Series–fixing scandal of 1919 had baseball been in such a sorry state of affairs. Back then, only the emergence of the larger-than-life slugger Babe Ruth won back the fans and restored the nation's faith in the game.

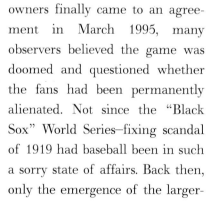

When baseball resumed in 1995, a decidedly un-Ruthian hero nudged the headlines of labor strife and fan revolt off the sports pages: Cal Ripken Jr., the workmanlike antithesis of the high-living, free-wheeling Ruth. But Ripken's modest demeanor and blue-collar approach to the game belied his compet-

Sammy Sosa (above) and Mark McGwire (left) treated fans to a summer slugfest as they chased Roger Maris's record.

Major League Baseball trademarks and copyrights are used with permission of Major League Baseball Properties, Inc.

"Permit me to congratulate Mr. Mark McGwire and to wish success to Mr. Sammy Sosa."

—*CZECH REPUBLIC PRESIDENT VACLAV HAVEL, when asked to comment on President Clinton's affair with Monica Lewinsky*

itive fire and genuine talent: He won two Most Valuable Player awards and made 12 straight All-Star appearances through 1994. Ripken came to work every day, and his manager penciled him into the lineup at shortstop every day, for 14 consecutive years. When the strike interrupted the 1994 season, Ripken had played in 2,009 straight games and was

within shouting distance of one of baseball's most hallowed landmarks: Lou Gehrig's record of 2,130 consecutive games, long thought to be unbreakable.

Many fans forgot their bitterness over the labor dispute as the entire country embraced a player whose devotion to excellence reminded them of why they came to love the game in the first place.

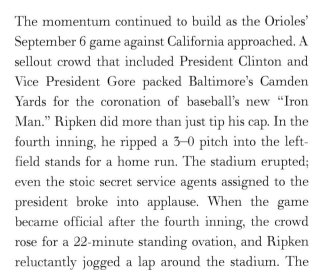

Cal Ripken took a lap around Camden Yards after breaking Lou Gehrig's record of consecutive games played (opposite); Sosa (inset and right), who was named MVP of the National League, almost single-handedly led the 1998 Cubs into the NL playoffs.

The momentum continued to build as the Orioles' September 6 game against California approached. A sellout crowd that included President Clinton and Vice President Gore packed Baltimore's Camden Yards for the coronation of baseball's new "Iron Man." Ripken did more than just tip his cap. In the fourth inning, he ripped a 3–0 pitch into the left-field stands for a home run. The stadium erupted; even the stoic secret service agents assigned to the president broke into applause. When the game became official after the fourth inning, the crowd rose for a 22-minute standing ovation, and Ripken reluctantly jogged a lap around the stadium. The 1994 strike had dealt baseball a serious blow, to be sure, but the fans' adulation for Ripken proved that the injury was not fatal.

If Ripken's achievement was a monument to steady hard work and determination, the 1998 home run derby between McGwire and Cubs' right-fielder Sammy Sosa was a tribute to herculean strength and grace under pressure. The season-long chase for the record between the hulking redhead and the ebullient Dominican captivated baseball like no other event in the sport's history. Fans arrived at ballparks hours before game time to watch batting practice; newspapers kept daily logs of the race;

and newscasts led off with McGwire-Sosa updates.

Despite their growing rivalry, the two men developed a genuine fondness and appreciation for one another. McGwire, weary of shouldering the media crush by himself, welcomed the eminently quotable Sosa into the fold. They began to feed off each other in a friendly game of anything-you-can-do-I-can-do-better. So it was appropriate that McGwire's Cardinals were hosting Sosa's Cubs on September 8. After McGwire cracked his historic No. 62, Sosa ran in from right field to embrace his friend.

The fun was far from over, though. McGwire had reached the mark first, but there was more baseball to be played and more home runs to be hit; the new record was still up for grabs. On the last Friday of the season, Sosa inched past McGwire with his 66th home run. He held the single-season home run record for 45 minutes, until McGwire responded with a homer that triggered a final power surge. In McGwire's last 19 swings of the season, he blasted five home runs, including No. 70 in his final at bat. Sosa had to settle for second place, with 66 home

McGwire acknowledged the St. Louis crowd's ovation (above) after belting his 70th home run of the **1998 season in his last at bat of the year (left) to top Roger Maris's record by nine.**

runs, but his heroic performance hardly went unrewarded. He won the league's Most Valuable Player award, and he propelled the Cubs into the playoffs for the first time since 1989.

At decade's end, baseball was the real winner. Ripken, McGwire and Sosa had helped erase the sport's ugly recent past. As Montreal manager Felipe Alou said after the '98 season, "You don't hear about the strike anymore. Sometimes, something has to almost die, like baseball did, for the miracle to take place. The average fan has more faith in the game now."

Aftermath

Cal Ripken finally decided to take a day off on September 20, 1998, when he voluntarily removed himself from the lineup against the Yankees. The Streak lasted more than 16 years and reached 2,632 games.

McGwire and Sosa immediately proved that 1998 was no fluke, chasing history yet again in 1999. Sosa belted 63 home runs in '99 to become the first player to hit 60 or more home runs in two seasons, but McGwire passed him at the wire again, finishing with 65.

VIRTUAL REALITY

Virtual reality is the twentieth-century equivalent to the wonderland that Alice discovered when she stepped through the looking glass—utterly convincing yet strangely surreal. Wearing wraparound goggles and using a wand or a mouse to navigate, a visitor to Crayoland—at the National Center for Supercomputing Applications in Urbana-Champaign, Illinois—can wander through a crayon house, splash in a crayon pond and dodge a swarm of bees in a crayon forest. As she looks from left to right, raises or lowers her eyes, the view and the perspective shift seamlessly and continually, just as they would in the real world. Stereophonic sound intensifies the illusion of reality.

Common sense tells the visitor who straps on the goggles and steps into the lightproof, 10-foot cube called the CAVE (for Cave Automatic Virtual Environment) that Crayoland is not real. But the fantastic real-time environment of computer-generated three-dimensional graphics convinces

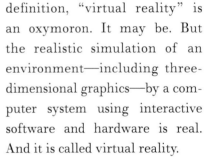

her of another, virtual, reality.

Physicists use the term "virtual" to describe images such as rainbows, reflections in mirrors and mirages that appear at a point in space where there is no actual object. Based on their definition, "virtual reality" is an oxymoron. It may be. But the realistic simulation of an environment—including three-dimensional graphics—by a computer system using interactive software and hardware is real. And it is called virtual reality.

Virtual reality technology took off in the mid-1980s, when NASA's Ames Research Lab in Mountain View, California, developed the Virtual Interface Environment Workstation—VIEW for short. This interactive system consisted of a "reality engine": a computer and its software; a head-mounted display with two miniature video monitors, one for each eye; and a sensor-equipped glove that allowed the wearer to signal the computer to modify the envi-

The mind-bending technology of virtual reality could simulate a game of pool (above) or a trip inside an RNA molecule (left).

ronment by moving his or her fingers. VIEW created virtual trips into space and enabled scientists to walk around inside computer models of molecules.

By the early 1990s the U.S. Army was staging vast virtual war games with its Simulated Network (SIMNET), which linked hundreds of players at far-flung military installations via high-speed telecommunications. One such virtual battle reenacted an offensive launched by the Armored Cav-

alry Regiment against Iraq during Desert Storm in 1991. Veterans of the offensive who took part in the simulation felt they were reliving the actual battle.

Sophisticated CAVE technology made its public debut in Chicago at a national conference of computer graphics professionals in 1992. Attendees lined up in the morning and waited patiently, sometimes for as long as five hours, to have a turn in the box, which featured an array of virtual

The possibilities of virtual realities, it appears, are as limitless as the possibilities of reality. They can provide a human interface that disappears—a doorway to other worlds."

—*SCOTT FISHER, of Virtual Interface Environments*

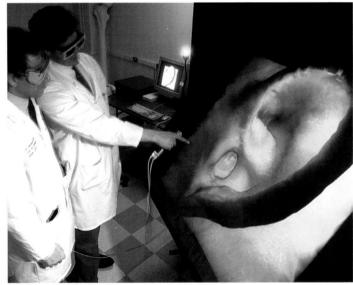

realities. But such VR systems are expensive—a CAVE total-immersion cube can top $1 million—and at decade's end most were still being operated by the government, the military and university research laboratories.

Nevertheless, a growing number of architects, engineers, designers and other professionals were taking advantage of this versatile tool to analyze data, review designs and solve problems. At the UCLA School of Architecture's Urban Simulation Laboratory, a virtual Los Angeles was being created that would eventually represent 4,000 square miles of the sprawling metropolis. Consisting of aerial and street-level photos that were digitally converted into three dimensions, the cyber-city accurately replicated not only large features such as buildings, parks, roads and bridges but also details as small as graffiti, trees and street signs. A user

could remove a group of buildings and replace them with a proposed development, then fly up for a bird's-eye view or drive down a street to evaluate the project's impact on traffic flow, appearance and other features of the existing neighborhood.

One company that bought into high-end VR was General Motors, which simulated car crashes in its two CAVEs. "We run the data to see if the engine is buckling and rolling under the feet of the people in the passenger compartments, which is what you'd like it to do in a head-on crash," said a GM research scientist. "With the CAVE, we can clip away the exterior and see just what we want to see."

While developing a design for the U.S. Joint Strike Fighter plane, engineers at Boeing tested a virtual prototype of the plane and discovered that when the landing gear was down the door of the weapons bay couldn't open all the way. Correcting the design error on a real plane would have cost millions of dollars. A Boeing manager commented, "If we hadn't caught that problem until production, we'd have had to pull the airplanes off the line." VR, he said, "is so much more than a blueprint because it is interactive."

By 1999 VR was the hot new technology in the entertainment industry. DisneyQuest theme

Virtual reality's applications ranged from the practical—General Motors's use of the technology for safety research and to hold virtual meetings (opposite)—to the playful—a virtual roller-coaster ride in Mississippi (left)—to the whimsical—a journey to the center of a compressed sponge (above).

parks offered such adventures as a virtual carpet ride and a trip to the Underworld using a stereoscopic VR helmet. Visitors to New York City's new Hayden Planetarium could leave Earth in a virtual spacecraft, fly past Mars and Jupiter, traverse the Milky Way and hear the sun rumble.

Futurists predicted a day when virtual reality would enter the home. A family would settle down at its computer entertainment center and with the flick of a joystick or the click of a mouse slip through the looking glass into a world of sights, sounds, sensations and even smells that seemed as real as the one beyond the front door.

Aftermath

At decade's end a new wrinkle in VR technology was in the works at the Human Interface Technology Laboratory at the University of Washington. Called virtual retinal display, or VRD, it eliminated the miniature monitors used to display computer-generated images. In their place, VRD used low-powered lasers to project the images directly onto the viewer's retina, producing sharper, brighter images than the best screen projection system could deliver.

SPORT UTILITY VEHICLES

America's affinity for the automobile stretches back to 1908 when the first Model T rolled off the Ford Motor Company assembly line. The automobile immediately symbolized wealth and freedom. And as the growing nation changed shape, so did its cars. What was desirable in the 1950s—a long, broad Cadillac with tail fins— gave way to the muscle cars of the 1960s—the sleek Mustangs and Corvettes. During the gaso- line shortages of the '70s, fuel- efficient economy cars like the Chevy Chevette gained popular- ity. Prosperity during the 1980s made two-car families the norm, and foreign lux- ury sedans like Mercedes and BMW became com- mon sights on American highways.

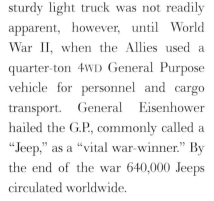

The car-buying public might have felt it had seen it all as the 1990s dawned. But as the auto- mobile entered its second century of production, sustained economic growth and a highly mobile, trend-loving society conspired to transform the humble, utilitarian four-wheel drive sport utility vehicle into an automotive must.

The first 4WD vehicle (meaning power is supplied to both axles) was made in 1904 by Amsterdam's Spyker Manufacturers. The usefulness of such a sturdy light truck was not readily apparent, however, until World War II, when the Allies used a quarter-ton 4WD General Purpose vehicle for personnel and cargo transport. General Eisenhower hailed the G.P., commonly called a "Jeep," as a "vital war-winner." By the end of the war 640,000 Jeeps circulated worldwide.

The Jeep was not the only 4WD vehicle in the civilian market for very long, though it would dominate the new sport utility vehicle category for a generation. To compete with the Jeep and capi- talize on growing consumer interest in outdoor activities, Ford introduced the Bronco in 1966, and Chevrolet unveiled the K10 Blazer in '69. Like the Jeep, both had all-weather, all-surface capabilities.

A descendant of the workhorse army Jeep, the SUV handled cargo (left) and mud (above) with equal ease.

Although sales of the gas-guzzling SUVs buckled in the early '70s under the pressure of fuel shortages, changes were afoot that would ultimately revive the market. Car companies began to produce SUVs with enclosed back-seats and cargo areas; subsequent models of this new "prestige" category offered automatic transmission and a choice of two or four doors. The Toyota Land-Cruiser touted such cushy features as power steering and air conditioning. By the 1980s manufacturers, who had all but forgotten the SUV's rugged wartime genesis, were upgrading the vehicles' interiors with larger seats and quality audio systems. They even tried to tame the SUV's bouncy ride by altering suspension systems.

Consumers happily endured the bumpy trip, abysmal gas mileage, notoriously poor handling and escalating sticker prices. The one millionth Jeep, a red Cherokee, rolled off a Chrysler assembly line in March 1990, ushering in the golden age of SUVs. Sales tripled from one million in 1990 to 3.1 million in 1999. No longer reserved for hauling leaves and grass clippings to the dump or towing the boat to the vacation house, the SUV emerged as an all-purpose alternative to the sedan. Parents transported kids to soccer practice; executives commuted to the office.

The middle class took advantage of no-money-down leases to choose from the similarly priced and styled Cherokee, Nissan Pathfinder, Ford Explorer, Isuzu Rodeo and Toyota 4Runner. High-brow suburbia tooled around in $43,000-Range Rovers with buttery leather seats, sun roofs and CD players. And Hollywood stars abandoned their trademark limousines: Arnold Schwarzenegger became one of the first civilians to own one of Chrysler's $56,000-extra-wide High Mobility, Multipurpose Wheeled Vehicles—a.k.a. the Hummer or Humvee. He drove the car to the *Termina-*

"They're called sport utility vehicles—odd, because sport, when attached to four wheels, means low, fast, and sexy, while utility implies down-to-earth and dull. Today's SUVs are neither, and their popularity is puzzling."

—CAR AND DRIVER MAGAZINE, *December 1999*

tor 2: Judgment Day movie premiere in July 1991.

By 1995 trucks and SUVs were outselling comparably priced luxury sedans in the U.S. market. To win back affluent baby boomers, Mercedes, Lexus, BMW and Lincoln all introduced SUV models by the late 1990s. "Everyone, it seems, loves sport utility vehicles," wrote Larry Edsall in *AutoWeek* in 1999. Indeed, in 1998 an estimated 20 percent of all U.S. passenger vehicles were SUVs—an impressive 65 million vehicles. "Manufacturers love the big profit margins. Buyers love the fashionable rugged looks, the way SUVs can carry them through seemingly any environment, how they provide the perception of safety and security, and how they offer spacious and versatile interior packaging." Ultimately, it seemed Americans loved their SUVs more for the wealth they symbolized than for the freedom they provided. Fewer than five percent of SUVs on the road in the late '90s would ever travel off road.

Aftermath

In the late '90s Ford and Chevrolet unveiled even longer, taller and wider beasts. These über-SUVs seated eight with room left over for luggage and pets.

Not everyone liked SUVs. Passenger-car drivers' views were obstructed by the high-riding vehicles with tinted windows, and while SUV drivers felt safe, sedan drivers feared collision. In 1998, Mercedes became the first SUV manufacturer to introduce collision-friendly lower bumpers.

In 1999 President Clinton announced that light trucks and SUVs would be subject to the same national pollution control standards as passenger cars. They had previously been exempt.

The new requirements were not expected to squelch SUV growth. At the close of the century, 42 different models graced showroom floors. Automakers expected that number to jump to 70 by 2004.

IMPROVING EDUCATION

In 1981 the Reagan Administration commissioned a comprehensive, 18-month study of the United States's public school system. The commission's final report, released in April 1983 under the title *A Nation at Risk*, was a scathing indictment of the country's education system. Citing "a rising tide of mediocrity that threatens our very future as a nation and a people," the report concluded with the strongest language imaginable: "If an unfriendly foreign power had attempted to impose on America the mediocre educational performance that exists today, we might well have viewed it as an act of war."

The landmark study jolted parents, educators and politicians from Washington, D.C., to Washington State into action, generating a ground-swell of education reform that intensified as the 1990s dawned. With the Cold War over and the Soviet Union dismantled, Americans were free to focus their attention on domestic issues. An era of unprecedented prosperity ensued and threw the problems that still vexed the public school system into even sharper relief. Why did American children consistently lag behind their industrialized-world counterparts in the most fundamental academic skills? Even more troubling—and highly relevant to education—how could 15 million children be living below the poverty line in the wealthiest nation on Earth?

The answers came fast and furious, and from all quarters. Raise the standards for teachers and for school curricula, cried some. Introduce

Classrooms full of eager students (left) were increasingly common in the late '90s, as were school computers (above).

Nearly 50 percent of U.S. classrooms had Internet access (opposite) by 1998, up from three percent in 1994; among the measures aimed at improving the U.S. educational system were the reintroduction of school uniforms (left) and the privatization of schools by such companies as the Edison Project (above).

vouchers for children of impoverished families to attend private schools, said others. Bring back school uniforms; institute charter schools that retain government funding if they achieve certain standards; let private companies take over the schools and whip them into shape. The list went on—and all the reforms were instituted in one form or another across the nation, with varying degrees of success.

A single, comprehensive solution had yet to emerge—indeed, the vast and complex problem is sure to persist well into the twenty-first century—but the piecemeal approach had already yielded results by decade's end. After falling gradually between the 1960s and the early '80s, standardized test scores have inched upward.

"Have we achieved all we set out to do? No, of course not. Are we moving in the right direction? Absolutely."

*—RICHARD RILEY, education secretary,
upon the release of the 1999 National Education Goals Report*

The average Scholastic Aptitude Test (SAT) math score, for instance, rose from 482 in 1995 to 512 in 1998. By the end of the '90s, African-American students were graduating from high school at the same rate as whites. These incremental improvements are both encouraging and indicative of how much work remains. Test scores still fall short of international standards, and African Americans still do not attend or graduate from college at a rate comparable to whites.

At a 1990 education summit the National Governors' Association adopted six National Education Goals it hoped states could achieve by 2000. President Clinton added two more in 1994. Objectives included a 90-percent high-school graduation rate, a first-place world ranking in math and science achievement, improved teacher

training and reduced crime. Not one of the eight goals was achieved, and in some cases there was regression. School safety declined, and only 17 states achieved a 90-percent high-school graduation rate. On the other hand, students at all levels improved in math, and more children began school in better health and with better reading skills than ever before.

Progress also was made in the preparation of preschoolers—the first goal of the 1990 summit. Programs like Head Start, created in 1965, seek to engage children at the earliest possible age and set them on track for academic success. While Head Start has been criticized as only moderately effective despite ever-increasing funding, the program has spawned other, so-called "model" programs that take the interventionary and preventative notions of Head Start even further, often beginning at birth. In a model program children typically spend the entire day in a stimulating, supportive environment where they engage in a variety of activities supervised by professionals who are certified in early childhood education. A long-term study that focused on one such pro-

With community volunteers (left) pitching in as tutors, and intensive teacher training (opposite) becoming more widespread, elementary school education was reinvigorated in the 1990s; first- and second-graders shared a one-room school in Vermont, where two promising young artists proudly displayed their latest creation (left, below).

gram, the Abecedarian Project in North Carolina, concluded that children who received comprehensive early preparation scored higher on cognitive tests, got better grades and were far more likely to attend college than children who did not.

Despite their expense—nearly double that of Head Start, according to one source—such holistic programs were gaining a toehold in the American educational scene at the close of the century and, it was hoped, would help boost the U.S. public education system in its climb back to excellence.

Aftermath

A record 53 million children were enrolled in public school in the United States in 1999, highlighting both the importance and the difficulty of education reform. With such a vast and diverse population engaged in the public school system, forging a comprehensive methodology for educational excellence was a daunting task at best. Yet those 53 million children represented the future of the nation, so the importance of educating them properly was obvious.

In opinion polls, voters regularly stated that improving public education was among their chief concerns. Despite the fact that education reform is largely a state and local government responsibility, it surfaced as a prominent issue in the 2000 presidential campaign, and each candidate weighed in with a series of varying proposals, ensuring that the increased public concerns and the gains made in the 1990s were a prelude to further improvements.

SEINFELD

"It's [a show] about nothing....Everybody's doing something, we'll do nothing." *Seinfeld*'s George Costanza uttered these words of wisdom to his friend Jerry Seinfeld as they prepared to pitch an idea for a sitcom to NBC. In a case of art imitating life, this short bit of dialogue from "The Pitch," an episode from the groundbreaking sitcom's fourth season, reflects the manner in which the show's co-creators, Jerry Seinfeld and Larry David, actually proposed their program to NBC. When all was said and done, Seinfeld, a standup comedian for 13 years, and his friend David, a former standup himself, delivered the funniest show about nothing that television had ever seen.

When it debuted in 1989, *Seinfeld* (then called *The Seinfeld Chronicles*) was a one-shot airing of the pilot, with no scheduled follow-up. But network executives were intrigued by the show, and in the summer of 1990 they aired four new episodes under the new title *Seinfeld*, and then rebroadcast the pilot. Set in New York City, with Jerry Seinfeld cast as a fictional version of himself, the show revolved around his life as a standup comedian and his relationships with his self-obsessed friends. In its first few years of existence *Seinfeld* endured six schedule changes and didn't score that well in the Nielsen ratings. But with its strong ensemble cast and witty dialogue, the show gradually developed a loyal following.

In February 1993, when NBC placed *Seinfeld* in its powerhouse Thursday-night lineup following the long-running *Cheers*, the program grabbed the attention of American viewers. After *Cheers* served up its final round of laughs in May 1993, *Seinfeld* moved into the plum 9:00 p.m. time slot. Once there, *Seinfeld* never finished below third in the Nielsens and was the No. 1 show for

The brainchild of Seinfeld and David (above, left and right), *Seinfeld* made brilliant use of its talented cast (left).

"Seinfeld" © 2000 Castle Rock Entertainment.

"Despite how different we were as individuals, we melded into this thing that worked more beautifully and joyfully than anything I will probably ever be part of again."

—JASON ALEXANDER

When they weren't in Jerry's apartment, Kramer, Jerry and the gang often reconvened at Monk's restaurant (above) to discuss their neuroses and foibles, of which George (opposite, left) was in no short supply; Wayne Knight (far left), who played Jerry's archnemesis, the postal worker Newman, brought a gleeful devilishness to the role.

both the 1994–95 and 1997–98 seasons.

The four memorable lead characters and consistently clever writing drove the show's success. Seinfeld came off as a carefree perpetual adolescent—he lacked a "real" job, always wore sneakers and was obsessed with Superman—to whom bad things rarely happened. If Seinfeld was a study in arrested development, his best friend Costanza, loosely based on David, was a case of severely warped

development. Brilliantly played by Jason Alexander, George could not hold a job and suffered through countless relationship problems, parents that bickered outlandishly and a vast storehouse of neurotic tics. Described in one episode as a "hipster doofus," Seinfeld's eccentric neighbor Kramer was played by Michael Richards, a master of physical, often slapstick humor. Former *Saturday Night Live* cast member Julia Louis-Dreyfus played Elaine

Kramer, who lived across the hall, made frequent and creative entrances to Jerry's apartment (right), where George and Jerry procrastinated while try- **ing to write their sitcom pilot (top); George's vituperative parents (above) often dragged him into the middle of their frequent disputes.**

Benes, Jerry's ex-girlfriend. Independent and opinionated, Elaine displayed an array of quirks and insecurities that made her one of the guys.

The writers of *Seinfeld* had a knack for mining mundane situations for comic gold. Episodes that hinged on such ordinary activities as waiting for a table in a Chinese restaurant, looking for a car in a mall parking lot or taking the subway were among the funniest. That said, the show often generated laughs from the most preposterous situations:

George and Jerry once took a ride in a limousine intended for someone else and were mistaken for neo-Nazis; George's fiancée, Susan, died after licking the envelopes to seal their wedding invitations—George, an inveterate tightwad, had insisted on the cheapest envelopes available, and the adhesive turned out to be toxic. The episode known as "The Contest" begins with George being caught by his mother, as she says, "treating your body like an amusement park." The four friends then wager to

Aftermath

When asked what she was going to do post-*Seinfeld,* Louis-Dreyfus exclaimed, "I'm going to sleep. I'm going to take a long, long nap." It was safe to assume, however, that more television and movie projects were in her future.

Both Richards and Alexander were slated to return to prime-time television, Richards on NBC in 2000, and Alexander for Fox in 2001.

Seinfeld took a brief vacation after his sitcom closed up shop and then returned to stand-up comedy. In August 1998 he performed on Broadway for an HBO special and a comedy CD. But by far the biggest change in his life was his marriage in December 1999 to Jessica Sklar, a 28-year-old publicist for the clothing designer Tommy Hilfiger. It was the 45-year-old's first foray into marriage. One can't help but imagine that Jerry's getting married would have made a great episode of *Seinfeld.*

see who can last the longest without engaging in, shall we say, solitaire. Sitcoms had certainly never broached *that* theme before.

Seinfeld also featured a hilariously idiosyncratic supporting cast, including Jerry's neighbor and arch-enemy, postal worker Newman (Wayne Knight); the belligerent soup chef dubbed the Soup Nazi; café proprietor Babu Bhatt; Crazy Joe Davola, and, of course, George's manic parents, Frank and Estelle (Jerry Stiller and Estelle Harris). The show also

coined several "Seinfeldisms," which became common parlance: "Master of your domain," "Yada, Yada, Yada" and the Soup Nazi's classic, "No soup for you!"

The final *Seinfeld* aired on May 14, 1998, and was watched by 76 million people. In the one-hour swan song, Jerry, George, Elaine and Kramer were jailed for failing to come to the aid of a mugging victim. Fans were left wondering what the four would do upon their release and what show could possibly fill that Thursday night slot with as many laughs.

EXTREME SPORTS

At the end of the 1990s more Americans than ever before were willingly jumping off concrete dams, risking life and limb on Mt. Everest, careening down hilly roads at 70 mph on street luges, diving from airplanes with boards strapped to their feet and launching themselves into 50-foot ocean swells.

The United States has a long history of envelope pushers—from the Wright brothers to Evel Knievel—but this explosive growth of extreme sports was enough to suggest some mysterious millennial fever, a Y2K bug or chronic *fin de siècle* ennui syndrome.

Or maybe it was simply a matter of thousands of kids spending hundreds of hours watching snowboarders, hang gliders and mountain bikers in awesome MTV footage, gnarly Mountain Dew ads, high-voltage X Games competitions on ESPN and extreme-sports cult movies like *Point Break*, *Terminal Velocity* and *Cliffhanger*.

Once the province of an elite group of athletes

dedicated to testing their limits against natural elements, extreme sports was transformed in the 1990s into a set of nontraditional sports practiced by pierced and tattooed youths with a penchant for utterances like "Are you afraid to die, or just to live?"

Much of what they did was a new variation on an old theme. Rather than skate along a paved path through a park for exercise, the extreme-sport in-line skater would spot a set of steps in the park, ride fakie (backwards) up to the handrail and descend the rail in a soul grind (the lead skate parallel to the rail, the rear skate perpendicular). Or, she might skip the park altogether and take a ride down a busy urban street clutching the bumper of a taxicab, a practice called skitching.

Not exactly the safest way to get from point A to point B, but not the most dangerous either. That designation would have to go to B.A.S.E. jumping. When bungee jumping became old-hat toward the

Whether they were scaling sheer rock faces (left) or sky surfing (above), extreme athletes played for maximum thrills.

"It's the Lewis and Clark gene, to venture out, to find what your limitations are."

—*JONATHAN SENK,*
adventure racer and former
army Ranger, 1999

Not content to merely in-line skate or bike down a path, extreme athletes took to sandstone rocks (right), performed stunts in Extreme Games competitions (opposite) or bungee jumped from sites such as the appropriately named Adrenalin Village above the Chelsea Bridge in London (above).

end of the '90s, inveterate thrill-seekers got their adrenaline fix by B.A.S.E. jumping. A usually illegal and always unforgiving form of recreation, B.A.S.E. jumping involves leaping from Buildings, Antenna towers, Spans and Earth. If a parachute malfunctions, there is no time to deploy a backup. In the 19-year history of B.A.S.E. jumping 46 participants have "gone in," or died. Yet at the end of the '90s more people than ever were trying it.

The obvious question asked by those who do not jump from tall buildings, climb Yosemite's sheer, 3,000-foot El Capitan without safety ropes or launch themselves into whitewater rapids in a small Tupperware-like craft for a round of "squirt-boating" is, *Why*? Freud might have answered, "death wish." Current pyschologists say, "Type T personality." A Type T person carries a "thrill-seeking" gene that requires him or her to work harder—or go to extremes—to register the effects of dopamine, a neurotransmitter that triggers feel-ings of pleasure and emotion. Type Ts, in other words, need excitement and novelty to feel alive.

Because the extreme sports of the '90s were all about pushing the limits and redefining boundaries, they constantly evolved. Skydiving, for example, added six new disciplines before the end of the decade. No longer content to jump from 15,000 feet, free fall and deploy a parachute, skydivers began sky surfing, free falling in formation and freestyling (aerial ballet). In a world that to some felt increasingly mundane—crime was down, the economy up—physical risk became life affirming.

Much of the innovation in alternative sports came from cross-pollination of various disciplines. Surfing and skiing begat snowboarding; skateboarding and luge combined to create street luge. Waterskiing and surfing merged into wakeboarding.

In the 1990s mountain climbing underwent an evolution of a slightly different nature. Since

81

Edmund Hillary and Tenzing Norgay conquered Mount Everest in 1953, the sport's equipment improved substantially, mountain routes were well charted, weather patterns scrutinized and all 14 of the world's 8,000-meter peaks had been "bagged." The most significant change, though, was that mountains became so accessible that many lost their aura of danger. Anyone with $65,000 to spend could sign on with a guide to retrace Hillary and Norgay's steps. Everest became so popular that on one day in 1993, 37 climbers vied for a foothold on the summit. Even disasters, like the 1996 expedition in which eight climbers perished, only seemed to heighten interest.

So what was a veteran extremist to do when precious few stones remained unturned, yet the desire to push the limits lived on? The Raid Gauloise, the most prestigious of the now myriad adventure races, was one option. Held annually since 1989, the race featured teams of five (including one woman) traveling hundreds of miles over seemingly impassable, often uncharted wilderness terrain. Competitors cut through jungles and traversed deserts riding everything from horses to kayaks in countries such as Ecuador and Madagascar.

It is safe to assume that, like George Mallory, who tried to climb Everest "because it was there," otherwise sane people will continue to sign on for adventure races, leap off bridge spans and hurtle down steep slopes on mountain bikes. As one extreme-sports Web site put it, "We take these risks not to escape life, but to prevent life from escaping us."

Snowboarding (opposite, above), the winter counterpart to surfing (above), grew by leaps and bounds in the '90s; skiers competing in ESPN's 1999 Winter X Games in Crested Butte, Colorado (insets), dazzled onlookers with an unending array of spectacular tricks and stunts.

Aftermath

ESPN's X Games have been so successful that NBC started up its own version, the Gravity Games, in 1999. According to the Sporting Goods Manufacturers Association, in-line skating is the most popular sport among children and teens. Snowboarding grew by 113 percent between 1993 and '98 to reach 5.5 million participants. Membership in the U.S. Parachute Association doubled during the decade.

Return to Space

One morning in April 1961, the nation awoke to find that the Soviet Union had succeeded in sending the first man into space. Yuri Gagarin's famed orbit spurred a fiercely determined President Kennedy to declare, "This nation should commit itself to achieving the goal, before this decade is out, of landing a man on the moon and returning him safely to Earth." With these historic State of the Union words and $1.7 billion to jump-start America's rocket program, a fledgling NASA began the uphill battle to space.

Dozens of elite pilots endured grueling psychological and physical tests before seven astronauts were chosen to serve in NASA's Mercury Project. (The best-selling 1983 Tom Wolfe novel, *The Right Stuff*, which became a popular film in 1983, chronicles their gripping story.) Of the seven, John Glenn, a World War II and Korean War fighter pilot of 149 bombing missions, became the first American to orbit Earth. On February 20, 1962, an anxious nation watched as Glenn orbited Earth for four hours and 56 minutes in *Friendship 7*, a capsule the size of a refrigerator. Walter Cronkite urged the Atlas rocket on with an impassioned "Go, baby, go" in his nonstop televised broadcast. Subway conductors informed their passengers of the rocket's liftoff and asked them to say a prayer.

The United States's position in the Cold War seemed to hinge on whether *Friendship 7* would survive the fiery reentry into Earth's atmosphere. When Glenn successfully splashed down southeast of the Bahamas, he became an instant American hero. A jubilant Kennedy greeted him in Cape Canaveral and four million New Yorkers threw 3,500 tons of ticker tape into the air to welcome the beaming Glenn back to Earth. With his proven patriotism, down-to-earth midwestern charm, devoted wife, Annie, and two children at his side, Glenn was a reminder of all that made America strong. Kennedy, worried about the political fallout should something happen to

Space pioneer Glenn (left, and above at a briefing after the *Discovery* mission) became the oldest person in space.

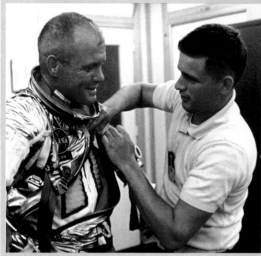

"Let the record
show: John has
a smile on his
face and it goes
from one ear to
the other one."
—*CURTIS BROWN JR.*,
Discovery commander,
shortly after takeoff,
October 29, 1998

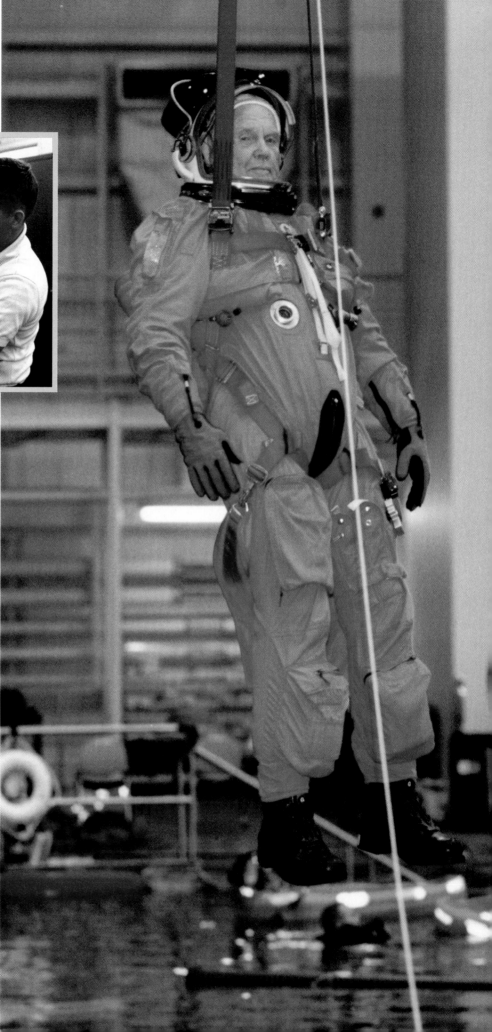

Though much had changed in the 36 years between his forays into space, Glenn's smiling demeanor while being suited up (opposite, inset, in 1962, and near left, in 1998) remained a constant; fortunately Glenn never had to execute the simulated parachute drop over water (opposite, right) during the actual *Discovery* mission.

Glenn during his reelection campaign, issued an edict—unbeknownst to Glenn—that the man who had become a national treasure was not to go up again.

By 1964 the earthbound astronaut became frustrated by his de facto PR position at NASA. When his requests for new flight missions were continually turned down, he retired from both NASA and the Marines to enter the business world. In 1974 Glenn successfully ran for Congress, where he represented his home state of Ohio as a popular Democratic senator until 1998. Thirty-six years would pass before Glenn returned to space.

In January 1998 NASA named Glenn to the crew of *Discovery STS-95.* As the oldest man ever to enter space, Glenn, at 77, would help scientists explore the similarity between the effects of aging and space travel. (The aging suffer many of the same ailments as astronauts: diminished bone and muscle mass, sleep and balance disorders and a weakened immune system.) While critics of NASA viewed Glenn's participation as little more than a publicity stunt, many scientists believed that anything that boosted the country's interest in the space program was worthwhile.

Much had changed since Glenn's first flight almost four decades earlier. In 1962 little was known about the effects of space and microgravity on humans. Scientists speculated that eyeballs might change shape or roll around in their sockets, while psychiatrists worried about a euphoric "breakaway phenomenon" that might prevent an astronaut from ever returning. The political climate, too, was vastly different: *Friendship 7*'s flight was a landmark in the fevered space race between the United States and the Soviet Union, whereas *Discovery*'s mission included the testing of parts for a joint U.S., Russian and Japanese space station.

The statistics of the two missions speak to the advances made in space exploration. *Discovery*'s flight lasted nine days to *Friendship*'s 5 hours. *Discovery* measured 122 feet to *Friendship*'s 10 and traveled 47 times farther and weighed 36 times more than its predecessor. Most telling perhaps, *Discovery* contained 2,312 cockpit controls and five computers while *Friendship* had 143 controls and no computer. As for comfort, *Discovery* astronauts never had to experience a G force (gravitational acceleration) beyond 1.6, whereas Glenn had weathered a highly unpleasant G force of eight in 1962.

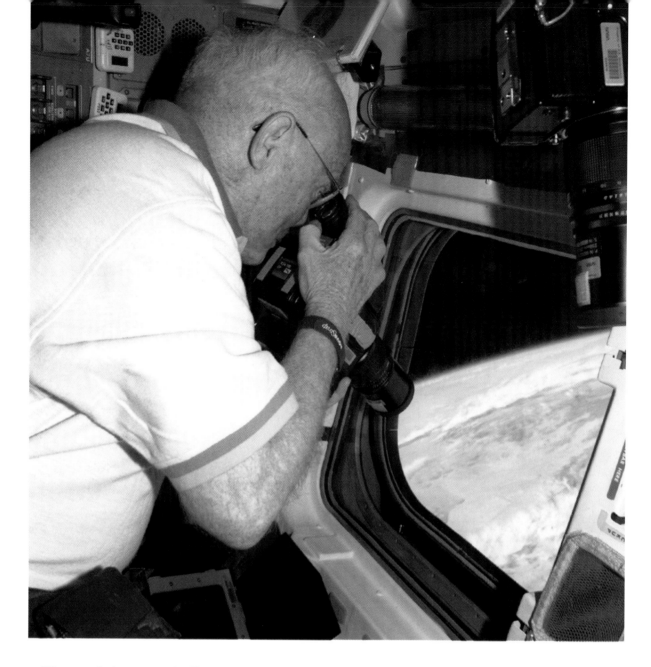

His second time around, Glenn was not the solo commander but a payload specialist among a crew of seven. He and Dr. Chiaki Mukai (his fellow payload specialist and the first Japanese woman in space) followed a rigorous daily schedule, participating in more than 80 projects. As one of the subjects of experiment himself, Glenn's brain-wave activity was continuously monitored while he slept. Each day, he swallowed a large jellybean-like capsule containing a thermometer that transmitted his body temperature throughout the day to a receiver on his belt.

On October 29, 1998, President Clinton, three of the original *Mercury 7* astronauts and thousands of reporters crowded Cape Canaveral. Another quarter of a million people lined the coastal Florida highways to witness the liftoff of the 92nd shuttle mission. Walter Cronkite emerged from retirement to cover Glenn's second flight, and the people of Perth, Australia, who had turned on their lights during Glenn's first go-around 36 years earlier, turned them on again. Several hours after liftoff Glenn radioed from orbit and echoed his famous words, "To use a trite old statement, 'zero-g and I feel fine.' " Glenn's flights stand as bookends to America's exploration in space: The first American to orbit Earth had become the oldest person ever in space.

Unlike his perilous journey on *Friendship 7* (left, below), Glenn's ride aboard *Discovery* was leisurely enough to allow him to pose with fellow crew members (left, clockwise from Glenn's left, commander Curt Brown, pilot Steve Lindsey, mission specialist Stephen Robinson, mission specialist Pedro Duque, payload specialist Chiaki Mukai and mission specialist Scott Parazynski) and to take some snapshots of his own (opposite) in commemoration of his groundbreaking effort.

Aftermath

Glenn's participation in the 92nd space shuttle mission placed NASA once again in the limelight as the astronaut commanded a Manhattan parade, a tour of Europe and Japan and countless meetings with heads of state. Glenn's contribution to geriatrics may simply have been to give it more glamour. But as 78 million baby boomers continue to age, living longer and better lives becomes paramount for Americans. Are the effects of aging—like microgravity—reversible? Only time will tell. But in the meantime, John Glenn has demonstrated that astronauts, too, can continue their careers well into their golden years.

COMPUTER ART AND GRAPHICS

When art and computer science joined hands in the 1940s, they formed one of the twentieth century's most prolific and synergistic unions. Initially a highly specialized tool for scientists and engineers, computer graphics—pictorial images produced on a computer—eventually entered the domain of artists who used this technology to visualize images and motion. By the 1990s every visual medium from video games to ATM machines employed computer graphics. Engineers and architects turned to computer-aided design (CAD) to construct space shuttles and skyscrapers. Filmmakers used computers to morph liquid metal into a man, as in *Terminator 2: Judgment Day,* or bring an entire child's room of toys to life with startling realism, as in *Toy Story* and its sequel.

In the mid-1980s computers became smaller, easier to use and more affordable. At the same time, desktop publishing software like QuarkX-press and Pagemaker began to revolutionize the way graphic designers worked. By clicking a hand-held mouse or typing a single keyboard command they could place and manipulate type, photos and color with laser-like precision in an electronic file.

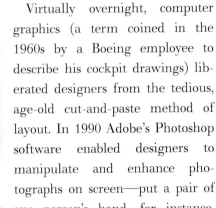

Virtually overnight, computer graphics (a term coined in the 1960s by a Boeing employee to describe his cockpit drawings) liberated designers from the tedious, age-old cut-and-paste method of layout. In 1990 Adobe's Photoshop software enabled designers to manipulate and enhance photographs on screen—put a pair of sunglasses in one person's hand, for instance, remove a cigarette from another's. Using Adobe's Illustrator or CorelDRAW, artists could put down smoothly curved lines and precise straight lines with a mouse-controlled pen tool. By 1999 more than one million publishers, both large and small, of books, magazines and newspapers used desktop publishing software.

Computer animation created the delightful special effects of films such as *Toy Story* (left) and *Forrest Gump* (above).

> ## "I remember the [Disney] execs asking me during the very first *Toy Story* discussions, 'You mean you could actually have these characters in the computer talking? Lip synching? Really?'"
>
> —*DAN PHILIPS, special effects artist*

Engineers reaped the benefits of the new work stations, too. Although CAD programs had been in existence since GM and IBM first employed them jointly in 1959, they did not catch on until the '80s. Everything from naval ships and the B-2 bomber to clothing patterns and a subway extension in London has since benefited from the ease and precision of CAD. Architects put their T squares and scales into semiretirement and designed homes, office parks and even entire towns on the computer screen.

Filmmakers experimented with the new capabil-ities as well. In 1982 a crop of movies with plots heavily relying on special effects—*Tron, Poltergeist* and *E.T.: The Extra-Terrestrial*—pushed the limits of the burgeoning computer graphics industry. More than half of *Tron's* backdrop—the innards of a video game—was entirely computer generated, as were the ferocious closet in *Poltergeist* and *E.T.'s* healing of a bleeding hand. Even classic films were affected by advancing computer graphics technol-ogy. In a process reviled by the Directors Guild of America as "artistic desecration," colorization transformed black-and-white films.

Sophisticated computer-aided design programs made possible not only the simulation of natural light (opposite) but also the creation of highly detailed **representations of homes (left) with a computer; the advances piqued the interest of architects worldwide (above) who incorporated CAD into their practices.**

The entertainment industry's escalating use of visual effects in film and television proved less controversial. On the small screen Listerine bottles swung Tarzan-like through an animated jungle. In Michael Jackson's 1991 music video "Black or White" a morphing technique melded one face into another. In 1999 visual effects artist Terrence Masson lauded Disney's animated blockbuster *Aladdin* as the film with the "most varied and complex use of computer graphics" to date.

Hollywood, its eyes planted firmly on a computer screen, never looked back. *Jurassic Park*'s photo-real carnivorous dinosaurs, *Forrest Gump*'s "cameo" appearance by President John F. Kennedy and *Twister*'s angry funnels and flying cows—each was a product in part or entirely of two- and three-dimensional computer graphics techniques. All became '90s classics. For James Cameron's 1997 big screen sensation *Titanic*, Digital Domain made the ocean flow around a docked reproduction of the ocean liner, used computer-generated passengers in aerial shots of the deck and called on CAD to map *Titanic*'s actual sinking.

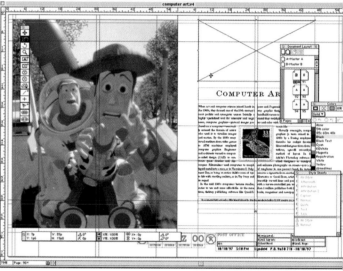

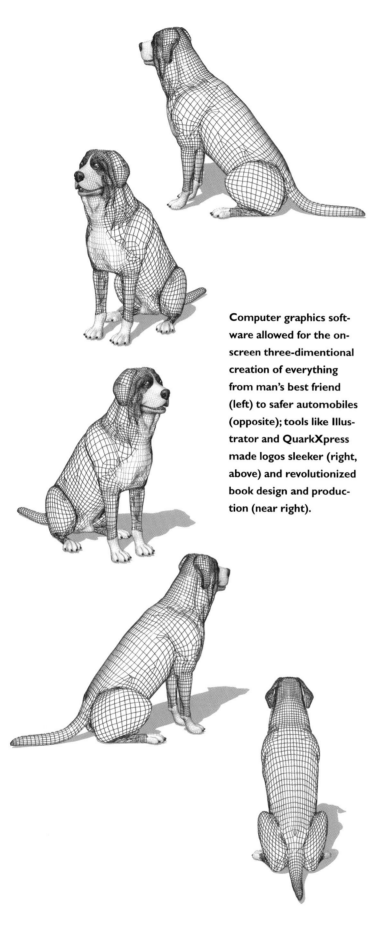

Computer graphics software allowed for the on-screen three-dimentional creation of everything from man's best friend (left) to safer automobiles (opposite); tools like Illustrator and QuarkXpress made logos sleeker (right, above) and revolutionized book design and production (near right).

Industrial Light & Magic—founded by George Lucas, writer and director of the *Star Wars* series—and Pixar—another Lucas creation now owned by Apple Computer mastermind Steve Jobs—set the standard for the use of visual effects in film. By the end of the century ILM was the largest digital production facility in the world. The company helped produce 1999's *Star Wars Episode I: The Phantom Menace,* which not only boasted some 2,000 special effects but also featured the first photo-realistic all-digital main character, JarJar Binks.

Proprietary animation software choreographed the characters' movements in each frame of the animated box-office hits *Toy Story* (Pixar, 1995) and *Antz* (Pacific Data Images, 1998)—a far cry from the old hand-drawn frame-by-frame days

94

of animation. *Toy Story*, its 1999 sequel and another Pixar animated feature, *A Bug's Life* (1998), became instant classics. Combined, the trio grossed $595 million in the United States and won critical acclaim for both visual effects and story content.

Proof, indeed, of the power of the computer graphics revolution. It transformed not only how professionals in publishing, engineering and entertainment performed their jobs but also the physical landscape of our society in the '90s. What was once coaxed out of pencil and paper now gushed forth from the ubiquitous computer—a device limited only by its master's imagination. As the century closed computer graphics stood poised to take us, in the words of *Toy Story*'s Buzz Lightyear, "to infinity and beyond."

Aftermath

With the advent of the World Wide Web and the Internet in the 1990s as vital sources for information and entertainment, computer graphics became increasingly important aspects of American culture. Web sites featured computer-illustrated "buttons" and other graphic elements to guide users. Unfortunately, Web surfers using computers with slow processing speeds often found themselves in a holding pattern as they waited for graphic goodies to download. Advances in file compression methods made the large image files, such as photos and short films, accessible to Web surfers with less powerful machines, proving once again that the liaison between art and computer science remains a strong one.

INDEX

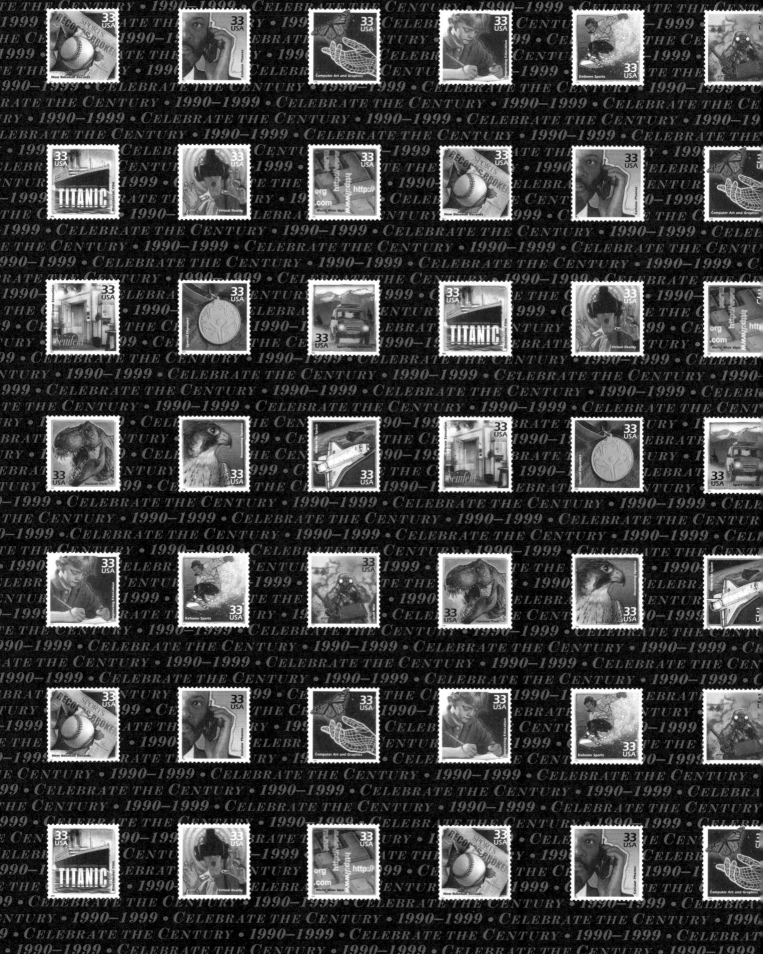